THE TIMELINE HISTORY OF THE
MIDDLE AGES

THE TIMELINE HISTORY OF THE
MIDDLE AGES

FROM 400 CE to 1500 CE

MEREDITH MACARDLE

WORTH
PRESS

This page: Medieval coats of arms form part
of a stained glass window.
Page 1: An illumination from a medieval manuscript.
Page 2: An illustration from *Les Trés Riches Heures du Duc de Berry*.
Page 3: A 14th-century fresco of young nobles at leisure.
Note: All borders and ornamentation used in
this book are of medieval origin.

First published in 2012 by Worth Press Ltd
Cambridge, England
info@worthpress.co.uk

© Worth Press Ltd, 2012

Text © Meredith MacArdle

British Library Cataloguing in Publication Data
A catalogue record for this book is available from the British Library

ISBN: 978-1-84931-044-4

10 9 8 7 6 5 4 3 2 1

Publisher's Note: While every effort has been made to ensure that the
information herein is complete and accurate, the publishers and authors
make no representations or warranties either expressed or implied of any
kind with respect to this book to the reader. Neither the authors nor the
publisher shall be liable or responsible for any damage, loss or expense of
any kind arising out of information contained in this book. The thoughts
or opinions expressed in this book represent the personal views of the
authors and not necessarily those of the publisher. Further, the publisher
takes no responsibility for third party Websites or their content.

The images used in this book come from either the public domain or from
the public commons unless otherwise stated.

Design and layout: Arati Devasher, www.aratidevasher.com

Printed and bound by Imago Publishing China

CONTENTS

THE NORMANS

Originally from Scandinavia, Vikings or Norsemen/ Northmen/Normans settled in northern France in 911, and a separate wave carved out a kingdom in southern Italy in the 11th century. From these two bases the Normans conquered England (from the Anglo-Saxons) and Sicily (from the Arabs) respectively.

THE VIKINGS

A map showing the holdings of the 8 "tongues" or divisions of the Knights Hospitaller (Knights of St. John) in the late 1300s, after the order received much of the property of the disbanded Knights Templar.

EUROPE DURING THE MIDDLE AGES

As the Middle Ages began, the huge Roman empire came under increasing pressure from "barbarian" tribes living on the north-eastern borders of the empire. Roman legions or armies were withdrawn to defend the Italian heartland, leaving the way clear for Germanic tribes to cross into western Europe and migrate into the south. During the "Dark Ages" populations criss-crossed the continent before settling down into new kingdoms such as the Visigoths in Spain, the Lombards in north Italy, and the Franks in France/Germany.

England was invaded by Angles, Saxons, Jutes, and Frisians from northern Europe, then, from what is now Scandinavia, Viking marauders later raided coastlines and river towns throughout the continent. These Northmen or Normans settled in regions as disparate as Kiev in Ukraine and Normandy in France, from where they invaded and conquered England. Normans also conquered southern Italy and Sicily.

THE ANGLO-SAXONS

GERMANY UNDER FREDERICK BARBAROSSA (REIGNED 1155–90)

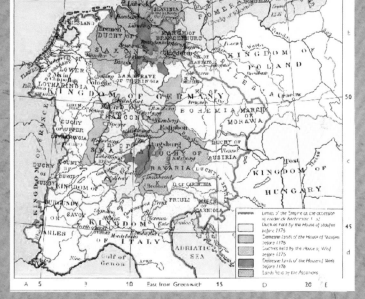

THE ROMAN EMPIRE C.150, NEAR THE HEIGHT OF ITS POWER

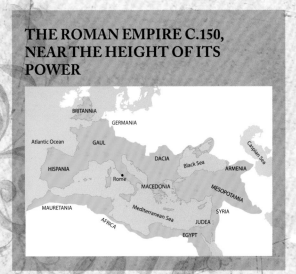

EASTERN ROMAN (BYZANTINE) EMPIRE C. 400 AD

THE ISLAMIC CALIPHATE 622–750

INTRODUCTION

It was a time of terrible savagery and yet the arts flourished. It was a period of invasions and migrations as different people criss-crossed the continent, while at the same time the foundations of modern, stable nations and society were laid. And, despite stagnation and ignorance for several centuries, important advances were made, such as the development of printing and of gunpowder.

The European Middle Ages or medieval period was a time of transition between the classical era of the great Greek and Roman civilizations, and the beginning of the early modern world. The term itself was first used in 1469 to indicate that the preceding centuries since the fall of Rome had been an "inbetween" time, an interruption of civilized progression from the classical period, a progression that was resumed in the late fifteenth century. By the late seventeenth century it was an accepted fact that history was divided into three stages: ancient, middle, and new.

As in all periods of history, there is no one, single starting date or finishing date, but the Middle Ages are generally held to cover about 1,100 years, from *about* 400 CE to *about* 1500 CE, from the final decline of the Western Roman Empire to the full flourishing of the Renaissance in Europe.

Many different dates are given for the beginning of the Middle Ages:

- Some historians argue that the Middle Ages began in 410 when the Visigoths sacked Rome.
- Others say that it began in 476 when the Germanic barbarians overthrew the last Roman emperor Romulus Augustulus and brought about the end of the Western Roman Empire.
- Yet others think that the year 500 is an acceptable beginning for the period.
- In Scandinavia, it is held to begin in the eleventh century, after Christianity took hold and written histories signaled the end of the "Prehistoric" period.

The end of the European Middle Ages is just as contentious:

- Some historians say that the fall of Constantinople in 1453 was the decisive event.
- Others hold that it was the discovery of America in 1492 …
- … or the start of the Reformation in 1517.
- Some English historians hold that the end of the Wars of the Roses in 1487 heralded the start of a new age …
- … while in Italy 1401 is often used as the demarcation. This is the year that one of Florence's most significant artistic events took place, when the new, Renaissance-style design for the "Gates of Paradise," the east doors of the Florence baptistery, were commissioned from Lorenzo Ghiberti (1378–1455).
- In Spain 1492, when the last Moorish or Muslim kingdom fell to Christians, is sometimes used.

This book covers from 400 CE to 1500 CE to ensure that all important events in the European Middle Ages are

Left: Falconry was a popular pastime for men and women.
Facing page: Hunting not only provided food for the table but was also a popular pastime. Medieval artists often showed castles dominating the landscape.

covered, while also providing an introduction to the historical epochs that came before and after.

Whatever precise date is used, the beginning of the Middle Ages was a time of great upheaval for Europe. The vast Roman Empire fragmented and much smaller states or local feudal lordships took its place, fighting with each other for survival in the new world order. Along with law and centralized social administration, the fall of the Roman Empire meant the disappearance of large-scale building projects such as the aquaducts, civic buildings, and massive city walls that had been a feature of empire. Projects such as these were not begun again for centuries. Long-distance trade practically disappeared,

THE HUNS

Hungary

THE MONGOLS

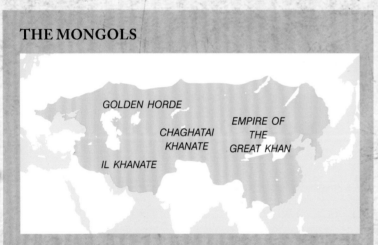

GOLDEN HORDE

CHAGHATAI
KHANATE

EMPIRE OF
THE
GREAT KHAN

IL KHANATE

CHRISTENDOM

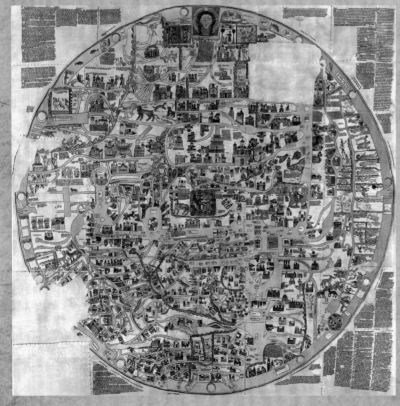

Medieval maps held the Holy City of Jerusalem to be the center of the world.

For most of the Middle Ages the Eastern Roman or Byzantine empire ruled many parts of eastern Europe. But waves of invaders from the east seriously threatened the empire. First the Huns swept through, giving their name to Hungary. Then the Mongols created a vast land empire stretching into eastern Europe. Byzantium was also threatened by the Arab caliphates that invaded and conquered Spain and Portugal. Eventually, the Roman empire succumbed to the might of Ottoman Turkey.

Most of today's European nations did not take shape until late in the Middle Ages, or even later. For example, the states of Germany and Italy did not unify until centuries after the Middle Ages. During much of the medieval period Europe consisted of small kingdoms which fought each other for territory or forged alliances, often through marriage. Even when larger nations began to form and a sense of national identity began to rise, the borders were usually different from the ones we know today. France, for example, was a smaller country than it is today, with independent states such as Burgundy and Brittany not yet absorbed.

Medieval people would not have thought of themselves as "Europeans" or as living in the continent of Europe. It is more likely that, if they considered themselves as belonging to any group other than their own state, they would have thought of themselves as living in "Christendom."

MOVEMENT OF THE GOTHS 3RD TO 6TH CENTURIES

Goths

Visigoths

Ostrogoths

Ostrogoths

Visigoths

INVASIONS OF VANDALS AND LOMBARDS, 3RD–7TH CENTURIES

Vandals

Vandals

Lombards

PROVENZA · ALVERNIA · FRANCIA · ITALIA · ARAGONA e NAVARRA · INGHILTERRA

ALEMAGNA

CASTIGLIA

POLONIA

HVNGARIA

VSTRIA

WALACHIA

MOLDAVIA

PONTVS EVXINVS

NATOLIA

MEDITERRANEVM

AEGYPTI PARS

ARABIA

SORIA

Jerusalem

and communities were thrown back on their own resources to develop independently.

During most of the Middle Ages Europe was a backward, unsophisticated region. The contemporary Chinese dynasties and other Asian societies were far more cultured, and Islamic empires in the Middle East and Spain were also far more advanced. New civilizations arose in Africa (Songhai, Mali, and Ghana) and in the Americas (the Aztecs and Incas), all while European states were becoming more fragmented.

But the Middle Ages did sow the seeds of the technology, the religious inspiration, and the national enterprise that brought Europe back to the forefront of world affairs. By the end of the period the Renaissance or "rebirth" was in full fling. This rediscovery of ancient knowledge and explosion of artistic endeavor helped take Europe from being a poor relation on the world scene to being on the forefront of global events, and completely transformed the future of the world.

PERIODS OF THE MIDDLE AGES

There are no firm, fixed dates for the different stages of the Middle Ages, but in general there are three separate stages:

- The Early Middle Ages / Dark Ages c.400–1000
  The term "Dark Ages" was coined by the Italian scholar Petrarch (1304–74) in disgust at the lack of Latin writings in those centuries. This period began with the collapse of Roman civilization in Europe and the fragmentation of society, with a move away from towns and cities. There was a concomitant scarcity of scholarship of all kinds, and long-distance communication practically came to a halt. As illiterate "barbarians" overran Europe, scholars thought that the light had gone out over the continent, and as recently as the 1800s some historians used the term "Dark Ages" to describe the whole of the Middle Ages.
- The High Middle Ages c.1000–c.1300
  During this period the ideals of chivalric Christianity were formed, with Christian-centered art, architecture,

Tournaments were a feature of medieval life.

and philosophy developing, for example the great Gothic cathedrals, representational painters such as Giotto (1266/7–1337), and Scholasticism. Literature from this period has survived in written form. Cities arose along natural trade routes such as the rivers Rhine and Danube, and nation-states began to emerge. It was also the period of the Crusades.

- The Late Middle Ages c.1300 onwards
  Europe experienced a crisis as the population was halved by famine and by the Black Death plague epidemic, the Catholic Church went through a traumatic schism, and revolts and warfare put an end to growth and prosperity. However, this final stage leading up to the Renaissance and Modern Era also saw the development of arts and sciences, with the introduction of printing, a renewed concentration on classical texts, and the beginning of the Age of Discovery. In Italy the Late Middle Ages was so closely linked to the early Renaissance that it is not considered a separate division of the medieval period.

CHANGES IN MEDIEVAL EUROPE

Although medieval Europe saw changes inspired purely from within, there were also immense influences from outside the continent. The Arab and Islamic worlds had several waves of impact, first of all with the Berber invasions from North Africa, which led to a Golden Age of civilization in the Iberian peninsula of today's Spain and Portugul, as well as temporary Islamic occupation of parts of the southern French coastline. Even after the Arab/Berber caliphs were driven from Europe, their influences remained, and then, once the Christian Crusades were launched to reclaim the Holy Lands in Palestine from the Muslims, the two cultures met again. Crusaders returning to their homes in Europe from the Middle East brought with them ideas and philosophies, as well as practical goods such as tapestries and metalwork.

Further afield, European culture came into contact with goods and ideas from India and China along the Silk Road, and from Africa along the long-distance trade routes north and south through the city of Timbuktu in modern Mali. At the end of the medieval period, of course, it was European explorers who began to influence the world, as the fall of Byzantium to the Ottoman Turks in 1453 meant that Europe was cut off from the Far East. In search of new routes to Asia, ships began to travel along the coast of Africa and round the cape to the Indies, foreshadowing Christopher Columbus's epic voyage to the Americas.

THE STATES OF THE MIDDLE AGES

For the sake of elegance, in the text of this book modern countries such as France and Germany are often referred to. Although in the medieval period their borders did not correspond to modern geography, it would be clumsy to be constantly mentioning "a region that became part of modern France," and so on. However, it is important to remember that the Middle Ages only laid the foundations for modern Europe: during those centuries the nations that we know now began to coalesce, but the boundaries shifted continuously throughout the period.

The Middle Ages also saw several important and influential states that have now vanished as independent nations, such as:

Burgundy
Flanders
Basque Navarre
Bohemia
The Papal States
Lands of the Teutonic Order
The Byzantine Empire

Conversely, some countries such as England that later played a major role in world politics as well as in European affairs were for most of the time in the background, not leading the way at all. It was a long period full of contrasts, and was far more complex and civilized than many later historians credited.

Pages from the *Book of Kells* and the *Lindisfarne Gospels*, two of the most beautiful illuminated gospels of the early Middle Ages.

401 Visigoths invade Italy.

402 Ravenna replaces Rome as capital of the Western Roman Empire.

410 Led by Alaric, Visigoths sack Rome. This event is thought by some historians to mark the beginning of the Middle Ages. ✿ Huns force Rome to give tribute.

406 Burgundian kingdom of Worms founded as Frankish peoples from Germany move into France.

425 By now more Germanic tribes from beyond the Rhine and Danube rivers begin to encroach on outlying parts of the former Western Roman Empire. They are being pushed westwards by the movements of nomads from central Asia such as the Huns. Frankish peoples arrive in Gaul (France), while Visigoths migrate through to Spain, Burgundians settle in parts of France, Lombards in northern Italy, and the warlike Vandals and Ostrogoths sweep down into the Mediterranean.

429 Anglo-Saxons begin to occupy southern England forcing the Picts and Scots to move further north in Britain. ✿ Vandals conquer Carthage in North Africa, and go on to take the Italian islands of Corsica, Sardinia, and Sicily.

433 Attila becomes ruler of the Huns, nomadic peoples who have settled east of the Volga River in Europe (giving their name to Hungary).

436 The last Roman army leaves Britain.

441–43 and 447–48 Attila the Hun attacks Constantinople, devastating the region, but is unable to besiege the city itself.

451 Huns invade Gaul but are repulsed at the battle of Catalaunian Plains or Châlons.

452 Attila the Hun invades Italy but withdraws before reaching the south.

453 Attila dies and his Hunnish empire fragments, never again representing such a threat to western Europe.

455 Vandals sack the city of Rome.

457 Anglo-Saxons take Kent in southern England.

405 Jerome completes his revised translation of the Bible into Latin, known as the Vulgate Bible.

411 St. Augustine writes *The City of God*.

432 St. Patrick starts his mission in Ireland.

430 Ninian is the first known Christian missionary in Scotland.

430 Death of St. Augustine of Hippo, the first great Christian philosopher.

◀ **The Theodosian Wall of Constantinople, now Istanbul.**

Attila the Hun rides over Europe. ▼

Early Middle Ages Most artists, whether painters or sculptors, are monks. Most art is commissioned by religious establishments.

403–13 New walls encircling Constantinople are built. Named the Theodosian Wall to honor Emperor Theodosius, at 4 miles long with a double wall and moat it is the largest defensive system in Europe. The wall is considered impregnable and is not breached until 1453 and the advent of gunpowder.

c.410 Alchemists, primitive scientists who merge superstition with chemistry, search for the Philosopher's Stone and the Elixir of Life.

452 The city of Venice in Italy is founded.

EARLY MIDDLE AGES (DARK AGES)

c.466 Birth of Frankish leader Clovis of the Merovingian dynasty (descendants of Merovech). He unites the Frankish tribes in areas of modern Netherlands/Belgium/France into a kingdom called Francia in Latin, and converts to Christianity.

471–488 Led by Theodoric, Ostrogoths establish a peaceful, racially harmonious kingdom in Ravenna, France, and he goes on to conquer northern Italy.

474–491 Zeno is Eastern Roman Emperor.

481–511 Wars of Clovis enlarge the kingdom of the Franks, partly by defeating the Visigoths of southern France.

476 The last Western Roman Emperor is killed by the German Odovacer. The "fall of Rome" is considered by many historians to mark the beginning of the Middle Ages.

495 Saxon Kingdom of Wessex in southern England founded.

c.500 Gaelic Irish people known as Scotti settle in the west of what is now Scotland and found the kingdom of Dál Riata (Dalriada).

493 Theodoric of the Ostrogoths marries a sister of Clovis the Frank.

c.503 At the Battle of Mount Badon (Mons Badonicus) the Britons, possibly under the semi-legendary King Arthur, defeat the invading Anglo-Saxons.

511 Death of Clovis, king of the Franks. His large kingdom is divided between his four sons, continuing the Merovingian dynasty.

The mausoleum of Theodoric the Great at Ravenna, built by him in 520 to serve as his future tomb. ▼

460–7 Principle of Papal Primacy determined by Leo I, that the pope has final authority over the Christian church.

491 The Armenian church splits off from Rome and Byzantium.

c.500–98 Life of St. David, patron saint of Wales.

494 Pope Gelasius I declares February 14th as St. Valentine's Day.

c. 504–70 Life of the British monk Gildas, who records the struggle against the Anglo-Saxons.

KING ARTHUR

A popular legend around the world, stories of King Arthur and the Knights of the Round Table began in the early Middle Ages. With exciting battles; brave knights; the shining city of Camelot; the mystical sword Excalibur; the clever wizard Merlin; the tragic three-way love story between Arthur, Guinevere, and Lancelot; the search for the Holy Grail; and the mysterious Isle of Avalon to which Arthur's dying body was taken, the legend has something for everyone and appeals to young and old. The myth has inspired countless books, many of them filmed as movies as varied as the musical *Camelot*, the Disney cartoon *The Sword in the Stone*, and the action-packed *Excalibur*. All these have kept the legend alive for new generations.

As an archetypal warrior-king, defending the land of Britain against Anglo-Saxon invaders, stories about King Arthur became mixed with general Celtic mythology, and were introduced into Welsh poetry. However, the contemporary account by the historian-monk Gildas does not mention his name. He first appears in history in the writings of Nennius around 830, *History of the Britons*, in which he is described as the war leader of the British kings, but some of his supposed exploits were clearly impossible. Fuller details of his life and legends were introduced by Geoffrey of Monmouth (c.1100–c.1155) in his *The History of the Kings of Britain*. King Arthur was romanticized by the chivalric poets, particularly by Chrétien de Troyes, who was court poet of Marie of France, Countess of Champagne, from 1160 to 1172, and he was further glorified by Thomas Malory's 1486 *Death of Arthur*. However, the historical reality of his existence is not yet confirmed.

The opening words of St Matthew's Gospel in the magnificent illuminated Book of Kells. ▶

5th century Illuminated gospels – illustrated hand-written Bibles with gold- or silver-leaf "illuminating" or "lighting up" the page are introduced in Britain and Ireland.

c.500 onwards For several centuries after the fall of Rome the Germanic tribes in northwest Europe are far less sophisticated than the Franks who have settled in Gaul and absorbed the Gallic-Roman culture. Despite the arrival of conquering Teutonic-speaking peoples, the Romanized inhabitants of France, Spain, Portugal and Italy maintain their cultural links with Roman civilization. This can be seen in the survival of their local "Romance" languages, derived from Roman Latin.

Medieval chronicle portraying the story of Sir Lancelot. ▶

c.500 Frankish/Visigothic etc invaders introduce new clothing styles of short tunics and leggings into the West.

511 Under the Merovingian dynasty, the system of law known as Salic Law is developed (named after the Salian Frankish tribe).

EARLY MIDDLE AGES (DARK AGES)

POLITICS, DYNASTIES, AND WARS

527–65 Justinian becomes Emperor of Byzantium. He reforms the economy, law, and the army, and re-conquers much of the Western Roman Empire, including Italy and North Africa. His wife Theodora, a former performer and courtesan, passes new laws giving women greater rights over property and divorce. She also makes rape a capital crime.

537 According to legend, King Arthur of Britain is killed at the battle of Camlann fighting the Anglo-Saxons.

568–86 Visigoths expand their authority throughout Spain.

Hagia Sophia in Constantinople, now Istanbul in Turkey. ▶

590–604 St. Gregory (I, the Great, also known as the Dialogist) is pope. He reorganizes the liturgy, sponsors Gregorian chants, sends out missionaries, and generally revitalizes the Church.

RELIGION

529 St. Benedict (480–543) founds an important monastery at Monte Casino in Campania, Italy.

532–7 Hagia Sophia in Constantinople is built by emperor Justinian. It is then the largest Christian church in the world.

550 St. David begins his mission in Wales.

565 Abbey of Iona on the Hebrides Islands off Scotland is founded by St. Columba.

587 In Spain the Visigoths begin to convert to Christianity.

589 The Italian Lombards convert to Christianity.

SCIENCE AND LEARNING

St. Gregory meets Anglo-Saxon captives in the slave market and determines to convert their people. According to legend he says "They are not Angles, but angels." ▼

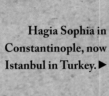

TRADE AND EXPLORATION

◀ **Mosaics in the Basilica of San Vitale, Ravenna, Italy.**

THE ARTS

526–48 Emperor Justinian builds the Basilica of San Vitale, Ravenna, Italy.

521 The Greek style of musical letter notation is brought to the West by the Roman philosopher Boethius.

Detail of musical notes for a Gregorian chant. ▶

perfeci ſh laudem pro

ter inimi coſtu os

590–604 Gregorian chant or plainsong is developed under the papacy of St. Gregory (I, the Great, also known as the Dialogist).

SOCIETY AND EVERYDAY LIFE

542 Early hospitals founded in Lyons and Arles in France. Medieval hospitals are run by religious orders.

c.550 Silkworms are smuggled from China, although the high-quality Chinese textiles are still luxury items.

580 Hospital founded at Merida in Spain.

578 Women are excluded from taking part in church choirs.

EARLY MIDDLE AGES (DARK AGES)

c.600 The Khazar kingdom forms between the Volga and Don rivers.

607 Byzantium defeats the Avars, a nomadic people who have conquered what is now Bulgaria.

610 Byzantine–Persian wars begin.

597 St. Augustine (the Apostle of the English) is sent by Pope Gregory I (the Great) to convert the Anglo-Saxon English. He bases himself at Canterbury, which becomes one of England's great cathedral centers.

609 The Pantheon in Rome is converted into a Christian church and the first All Saints' Day or All Hallows' Day celebration takes place there.

620 Norse invaders conquer parts of Ireland.

626 Avars lay siege to Constantinople while the Byzantine armies are on campaign, but fail to take the city.

627 Battle of Nineveh. Byzantium crushes Persian forces, and Emperor Heraclius awards himself the Persian royal title of King of Kings.

629 Visigoths take control of almost the entire Iberian peninsula.

636 Battle of Yamouk. Invading Muslims defeat Byzantine forces and take Syria. Jerusalem falls the following year and Egypt is conquered two years later. Within ten years, the Byzantines will lose nearly all their provinces in the East, keeping only a toehold in Anatolia.

633 Lindisfarne Monastery is founded on Holy Island off the northeast coast of England.

650 The tenets of Eastern Orthodox Christianity develop.

646 The Byzantine navy recaptures Alexandria in Egypt.

661 The oldest Visigothic church in Spain, San Juan de Banos, is founded in the province of Palencia.

664 Synod of Whitby. The British Celtic Church decides to accept the tenets of the Latin Church of Rome, and the Celtic Christian Church begins to disappear.

The cloister arches of Canterbury cathedral. ▲

600 The long-distance trade network spreads an outbreak of smallpox from India through China, Asia Minor, and to southern Europe.

619 John Moschus dies in Rome after completing his book *The Spiritual Meadow*, an account of his travels in the Byzantine Empire. As well as recording the lives of ordinary people, he describes a world where miracles are commonplace, monks live in desert caves, and anchorites make their homes on the summits of pillars.

▲ Carved figures of churchmen from Lough Erna, Ireland, showing the distinctive Celtic style of carving.

A typical Celtic Cross. ▶

7th century The *Origo Gentis Langobardorum*, outlining the history of the Lombard peoples, is compiled. The first fortification that will become Foix Castle in France is built.

6th–8th centuries Slavic peoples from eastern Europe migrate further west.

c.600 The phrase "God Bless You" in response to a sneeze becomes common, as plague rages through Europe.

▲ Foix Castle today. It was built on the site of 7th-century fortifications.

c.650 The population of Europe is about 18 million.

EARLY MIDDLE AGES (DARK AGES)

POLITICS, DYNASTIES, AND WARS

673 Civil war in the Frankish kingdom follows the death of Childeric II, king of Austrasia.

675 The first Bulgarian empire is founded south of the Danube.

685 At the Battle of Nechtansmere, the Scottish Picts defeat the invading Northumbrians.

686 With the victory of Pepin the Younger at Testry, he rules the Frankish kingdom as "Mayor of the Palace."

c.686/8 Birth of Pepin's son Charles Martel (the Hammer) in what is now France. He later becomes "Mayor of the Palace" under the Merovingian kings.

691 Clovis III becomes king of all the Franks.

696 Venice in Italy appoints its first doge (chief magistrate and leader of the city-state), Paoluccio Anaffesto.

711 Arab/Berber conquest of the Iberian Peninsula begins. The conquerors call their territory al-Andalus (land of the Vandals).

720 Arabs from Spain begin to take over parts of southern France.

719 St. Boniface begins his mission to convert Germans.

732 Battle of Tours (Poitiers). Charles Martel defeats Muslims and stops Berber/Arab advance into western Europe.

c.740 Some Russians adopt Judaism.

730 Iconoclast Controversy convulses the Byzantine empire. Emperor Leo III orders the removal of religious images and icons from churches and state buildings. Although ordinary people see icons as a way of gaining direct communion with the Divine, the army supports Leo's iconoclasm.

RELIGION

673 The first synod of the English church meets at Hereford. ❀ Ely Cathedral in east England is begun.

690 The English missionary Willibrord begins to convert the Frisians (in modern Netherlands).

SCIENCE AND LEARNING

Early Middle Ages Religious groups, whether attached to monasteries or not, run hospitals.

673 Greek Fire, an inflammable liquid made from saltpeter and resin is invented by the Syrian engineer Kallinikos. Projected from a hand-powered siphon, Greek fire can burn on water and is seen as the superior weapon of the age.

TRADE AND EXPLORATION

Late 7th century The market fair set up by the Merovingian king Dagobert at St Denis, near Paris in France, becomes an important link in a north European trading circle.

An Eastern Orthodox icon. ▶

THE ARTS

700 The Lindisfarne Gospels are created in England.

Early medieval art often focused on religious themes. ▼

731 The Venerable Bede writes his *Ecclesiastical History of the English.*

Charlemagne depicted on a stained glass window in Chartres cathedral. ▶

SOCIETY AND EVERYDAY LIFE

720 Islamic settlers arrive in Sardinia and in southern France.

751 With the election of Charles Martel's son Pepin the Short, supported by the Pope, the Merovingian rule of France comes to an end and the Carolingian dynasty begins (meaning descendants of Carolus, or Charles).

755 The last survivor of the Arab Ummayad dynasty, Abd-al-Rahman flees from Damascus to Spain and begins to establish a new kingdom, later caliphate, centered on Cordoba. An Arab Golden Age begins there.

754 Martyrdom in Frisia of St Boniface, apostle to the Germans.

771 Pepin's son Charlemagne or Charles the Great (768–814) unites the Frankish kingdoms of central France, most of Germany, and northern Italy.

778 Charlemagne defeated at the battle of Roncesvalles by the Vascons. According to legend, the knight Roland is killed here.

779 Offa of Mercia claims to be king of all England. He builds a defensive dyke along the border with Wales.

▲ **Charlemagne, the first Holy Roman Emperor and one of the towering figures of the Early Middle Ages.**

789 First recorded raid by Vikings from Norway on the British Isles, in Portland, Dorset, England.

The sight of a Viking longship such as this would have terrified the inhabitants of northern Europe. ▼

CHARLEMAGNE – CHARLES THE GREAT (c.740–814)

Considered to be "The First Knight" and a major figure of the early Middle Ages, Charlemagne is thought to have been born near Liège in what is now Belgium. His father was Pepin the Short, the first Carolingian King of the Franks. When Pepin died in 768, the kingdom was divided between Charlemagne and his younger brother, Carloman, who died suddenly in 771.

Now sole ruler, Charlemagne expanded his territories all over Europe, defeating invaders and bringing peace. His military leadership and strategies, as well as organization of continuous food supplies instead of ad hoc foraging for his army, inspired astounding discipline and loyalty in his troops and knights, and defined how the "perfect knight" should be. He was not, however, kind to pagans – they were slaughtered if they did not convert to Christianity or leave their territories. In 800, he defeated a rebellion against Pope Leo III who promptly crowned him Emperor of the Romans (the first Emperor of the Holy Roman Empire).

An intelligent and enlightened man in many ways, Charlemagne reformed the tax, administration, and legal systems; standardized weights and measurements; and established a great library of Christian and classical works. When he died he left an immense legacy that influenced the whole of Europe. Many consider that the era of the medieval knight began with him.

787 Second Council of Nicea. This important religious gathering settles many points of Christian doctrine. It is the last council accepted by both Eastern Orthodox and Roman Catholic churches.

8th century The first monastic community is established on Mont-Saint-Michel, France.

▼ **The interior of Cordoba's Great Mosque.**

775 In the "Carolingian Renaissance" under Charlemagne, beautiful illuminated manuscripts are produced in France/Germany.

8th–11th centuries The oral poem *Beowulf* is created in Old English.

784 Work begins on the Great Mosque at Cordoba, Spain.

Édité par
la CHOCOLATERIE D'AIGUEBELLE
Monastère de la TRAPPE (Drôme).

Soumission des Saxons à CHARLEMAGNE

Charlemagne in battle against pagans. ▲

782 Attacks by the Welsh into the English kingdom of Mercia are so common that the Mercian king Offa builds the defensive Offa's Dyke against them.

EARLY MIDDLE AGES (DARK AGES)

POLITICS, DYNASTIES, AND WARS

793 Vikings raid the Holy Island of Lindisfarne off the northeast coast of England. They then raid coasts of France and Spain.

795 Vikings raid the island monastery of Iona off Scotland, go on to establish a kingdom in northern Scotland; invade Ireland and create a kingdom there centered around the city of Dublin.

797–802 Empress Irene becomes the first female ruler of the Byzantine Empire. Ruthless in the extreme, she has her own son, Constantine, the rightful heir to the throne, blinded and thrown into prison. He soon dies in mysterious circumstances. Irene improves relations with the Vatican and allows the return of icons and sacred images in churches and state buildings.

800 After Charlemagne travels to Rome to support the pope against his enemies, on Christmas Day, Pope Leo III crowns Charlemagne the first Holy Roman Emperor, ruling a new Western Roman Empire. He presides over a centralized state with a revival of arts and culture.

c.800 Charlemagne takes over the region called Ostmark (Eastern March) in the Danube valley. The name evolves into Austria. He goes on to subdue the Saxons in southern Germany, and eventually rules France, Belgium, the Netherlands, northeast Spain, north Italy, and most of Germany, Austria, and Switzerland.

806 Third Viking raid on Iona. Surviving monks flee to Kells in Ireland, taking with them the illuminated manuscript the *Book of Kells*.

807 Byzantium and the Frankish kingdoms go to war.

813 When Charlemagne appoints his son Louis as co-emperor at Aachen, the pope does not attend. Power has devolved to the Holy Roman Emperor.

814 Death of Charlemagne.

826 Arab conquest of Crete and excursions into Greece.

Distinctive Viking art was widely traded. ▶

Portrait of John the Evangelist from the Book of Kells. ▼

RELIGION

8th century The first church is built at Westminster, London.

813 The remains of St. James are found by a miracle at Compostela, Spain.

SCIENCE AND LEARNING

▲ **Aachen Cathedral, the oldest cathedral in northern Europe and the place of coronation for German kings until 1531.**

TRADE AND EXPLORATION

800 The Arab caliph Haroun al-Rashid of Baghdad sends an embassy to Charlemagne.

800s Vikings trade along the Volga, Dnieper, and Dvina rivers between the Baltic, Black, and Caspian seas.

During the Middle Ages, cultures would merge together, as shown in this illustration of the Christian story of Noah's Ark in the form of a Viking ship with characteristic dragon prow. ▶

THE ARTS

796 Charlemagne builds an impressive church at Aachen (Aix-la-Chapelle) modeled on the San Vitale in Ravenna, Italy.

c.800 The *Book of Kells*, a magnificent illuminated manuscript, is created by Celtic monks in Ireland. ❧ One of the period's great sculptures, the St Andrew's sarcophagus, is created in Scotland.

800 Muslim Spain sees Arabs and Jews working together to translate Classical Greek texts and develop philosophy, science, literature, theology, and the arts.

c.814 After the death of Charlemagne, the Frankish monk Einhart writes an important Early Medieval text, a biography of the king, *Vita Karoli Magni*.

SOCIETY AND EVERYDAY LIFE

794 St. Albans Hospital is founded in England.

c.800 Jewish Golden Age in Muslim Spain begins.

800–1300 Medieval Warm Period – the North Atlantic region enjoys a slight overall temperature rise.

◀ **The opening of St. Luke's Gospel in the Book of Kells.**

EARLY MIDDLE AGES (DARK AGES)

834–45 Vikings raid northern France and northern Germany.

840 On the death of Charlemagne's son Louis the Pious, Louis's 3 sons fight over the division of the kingdom. Slavs in central Europe form a confederation.

843 With the Treaty of Verdun the Frankish kingdom is formally divided. Charles II, the Bald takes parts of modern France; Louis I, the German takes parts of modern Germany; Lothair I takes parts of modern Italy and Lorraine. So, the Carolingian Empire dissolves to form forerunner kingdoms of France, Germany, and Italy, although the Rhineland provinces are frequently causes of contention. The Gael Kenneth I MacAlpine becomes first king of united Scotland after defeating the Picts.

844 Arab forces destroy the Venetian fleet and penetrate as far north as Rome.

849–99 Life of Alfred the Great, king of Wessex in England. He codifies laws, promotes literacy and education, reorganizes the army, and fights off Danish invasions.

859 Norse pirates pillage the Mediterranean coast.

862 Rus Vikings capture Kiev.

865 Viking "Great Army" invades northern England.

867 Vikings establish the Kingdom of Jorvik centered around York in northern England. From there they attempt to widen their kingdom.

886 After initial defeats, Alfred the Great of Wessex/England defeats the Danish Vikings and agrees to divide the country between Wessex in the West and the "Danelaw" along the eastern coast.

c.895–900 Magyars conquer Hungarian Plain and later overrun Austria.

Alfred the Great. Having fled the Danes he takes refuge in an ordinary household, but, deep in thought, allows the cakes to burn. ▶

830 Christianity spreads into Scandinavia.

832 The library at the abbey of St. Gall in St. Gallen, Switzerland is founded. It becomes a major center of scholarship and learning.

late 800s The Greek Byzantine brothers St. Cyril and St. Methodius bring Christianity to the pagan Bulgars and Slavs. St. Cyril devises the Glagolitic alphabet in order to translate the Bible in Slavonic.

Reconstruction of the interior of a Viking hall. ▶

9th century The *Anglo-Saxon Chronicle*, recording the history of the Anglo-Saxons in England, is compiled in the kingdom of Wessex ruled by Alfred the Great.

VIKING CULTURE

Vikings are often thought to be nothing but barbarians, a primitive pagan people who survived by raiding other more cultured communities. Images of berserker warriors and longboats bristling with spears were the common idea of the Norsemen.

However, as well as preying upon other people, the Vikings did develop their own art forms, had a tradition of oral storytelling, a developed view of the universe, and laws giving rights to every level of society.

The name Viking perhaps originally meant a seaman from the Vik region of the fjord of Oslo in Norway, but by about 1000 it was used for all Scandinavian raiders from the sea. Vikings were only part-time pirates: most of the year they tended their crops or herds, or fished for a living. But, as summer approached, a warlord or chieftain would call for a crew and set sail to plunder, trade, or explore.

862 Foundation of Novgorod in Russia.

9th century "Carolingian Renaissance." Under Charlemagne and his descendants there is a period of political stability over a large area and resultant cultural growth. It is common among Anglo-Saxon communities for expensive and favorite items of clothing to be carefully itemized and allocated in a will.

c.885 Prague is founded in what is now the Czech republic.

EARLY MIDDLE AGES (DARK AGES)

POLITICS, DYNASTIES, AND WARS

▼ **Cluny Abbey, founded in 909.**

918 Death of Alfred's daughter Aethelflaed, "Lady of the Mercians", who reconqueres part of the Danelaw.

919 In the eastern Frankish lands (Germany) a new dynasty is elected, the Saxon Henry I who founds the Ottonian dynasty. He rules 4 duchies: Franconia, Bavaria, Saxony, and Swabia, along with Lorraine which is claimed by both the eastern and western Franks. These are the "stem" duchies.

937 Battle of Brunanburh. Having already defeated Welsh kings, Athelstan, king of Wessex defeats a Viking/Scottish invasion force and becomes first true king of all England.

954 The last Viking king of Jorvik in England, Eric Bloodaxe, is ousted.

955 Battle of Lechfeld. Otto I of Germany (the Great) defeats the Magyars and takes over Austria.

962 Otto the Great (912–73), king of Germany, is crowned Holy Roman Emperor. He re-unites the eastern and western Frankish lands into a powerful, prestigious polity, and begins the tradition that the elected German king is also Holy Roman Emperor as long as the Pope crowns him.

966 Duke Mieszko I converts to Christianity and founds Poland as a separate Slavik nation, recognized by the Pope.

◄ **Otto I of the Holy Roman Empire.**

RELIGION

909 The Abbey of Cluny is founded in Burgundy (now Saône-et-Loire, France). Within two years it introduces two developments: subordinate "daughter" monasteries, and the acknowledgement of papal authority over monasteries that circumvents all local disputes.

961 Monastery on Mount Athos, Greece founded.

SCIENCE AND LEARNING

TRADE AND EXPLORATION

BRITANNIA SAXONICA.

THE ARTS

ANGLO-SAXON BRITAIN

The centuries following the end of the Roman occupation of Britain up until the Norman conquest in 1066 saw England invaded and occupied by Angles, Saxons, Jutes, and Frisii, people from the regions of modern Germany and Denmark who were usually grouped together under the name "Saxons."

In the eighth century the term Anglo-Saxon was used to differentiate the British and the German Saxons, and by then the British settlers were using the term Anglii or English for themselves. Anglo-Saxons adopted Christianity in the seventh century and formed several distinct kingdoms within Britain. They had to fight off new invaders in the form of the Vikings and Danes, and in 1066 the last Saxon king, Harold Godwinson, lost the land to the Normans under William the Conqueror.

◄ **Anglo-Saxon helmet found at the Sutton Hoo ship-burial in eastern England.**

A stained-glass image of the Mercian saint Chad. ►

◄ **Anglo-Saxon Britain.**

SOCIETY AND EVERYDAY LIFE

950 onward Jews spread out in Ashkenaz (modern France and Germany in western Europe).

983 Great Slav Revolt: Slavs of Eastern Europe join with Danes to fight their Saxon (German) conquerors. They halt the eastern advance of the Holy Roman Empire.

987 Hugh Capet displaces the Carolingian dynasty in France and establishes the Capetian dynasty until 1328.

King Canute shows that he cannot hold back the tide. ▶

1018–35 Reign of Danish king Canute (Cnut) in England. According to legend, he proves to sycophantic advisers that he is not able to turn back the ocean tides.

1018 Malcolm II of Scotland establishes the Scottish–English border at the River Tweed. Lands within "the Borders" change hands frequently over the centuries and are subject to clans' feuds and raids.

1019 Yaroslav of the Viking kingdom in Russia turns Kiev into a Byzantine city with a monastery, a cathedral, city works, and a law code.

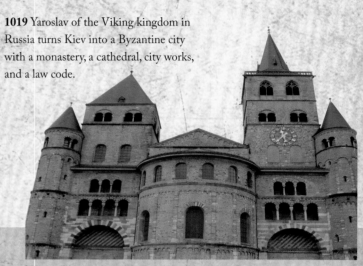

980 Scandinavian monarchs begin to convert to Christianity.

988 With baptism of Vladimir the Great, prince of Kiev, Russia or Kievan Rus begins to convert to Christianity.

10th century Most popes are corrupt and/or incompetent. Many church officials are also corrupt and unqualified.

1021–85 Life of Gregory VII (pope from 1083), church reformer.

▲ **Trier Cathedral is the oldest cathedral in modern Germany.**

998 An Anglo-Saxon teaching tool created by the monk Aelfric of Eynsham provides information about the tasks of many working people such as smiths, shepherds, bakers, ploughmen, salters, carpenters, cobblers, huntsmen, and fowlers.

◀**Danish weapons of the 10th century.**

c.1001 The Persian polymath Avicenna (Ibn Sina) writes *The Canon of Medicine*, which was widely adopted in Europe as a medical textbook.

1021 The Arab scholar Ibn al-Haytham (Alhazen) publishes his groundbreaking work *The Book of Optics*, which is later translated into Latin and influences European scientists.

c.1022–c.1058 Life of Solomon ibn Gabirol, the Spanish Jewish poet and philosopher.

c. 980 Norwegians under Eric the Red settle on Greenland.

c.1000 Under Leif Ericsson (son of Eric the Red), Vikings make first European landing in North America and found the settlement of L'Anse aux Meadows in Canada.

12th century The legend of Prester John arises. Supposedly a Christian king of Ethiopia, it is popularly held that his realm holds fabulous treasures including the fountain of youth.

11th century In the "Great Clearances," people begin to re-explore many areas north of the Alps that had been abandoned to nature since the fall of Rome. Whole forests are cleared for cultivation and settlement.

11th and 12th centuries Warmer temperatures mean harvests are good, there is less famine, and there is a surplus of crops for trade. New mercantile links are forged.

c.1000 The predominant artistic style is Romanesque, with architecture encompassing earlier Roman features such as rounded arches and barrel vaults, and with Byzantine influences in sculpture, painting, metal- and enamel work.

1016–35 King Canute begins work on the Palace of Westminster in London. It becomes the Houses of Parliament.

1019–47 Trier Cathedral is built in Germany, incorporating an earlier Roman temple on the site.

c.1020 The 8th-century abbey church of Mont-St-Michel, France is replaced by the present-day Romanesque complex.

◀**The straight lines of a Romanesque church.**

1000 The population of Europe is about 36 million.

c.1000 This date is held by many historians to mark the end of the Dark Ages.

◀ **Mont-St-Michel. A church has stood on the site since the 8th century.**

HIGH MIDDLE AGES

POLITICS, DYNASTIES, AND WARS

1031 Ummayad caliphate in Spain collapses. Small, divided states take its place.

1032 The Duchy of Burgundy is formed, partly from lands belonging to the second Kingdom of Burgundy. Dukes of Burgundy from then on are relatives of the kings of France, sometimes challenging the French rulers.

1040 Macbeth takes control of Scotland. Although a good king, he is demonized centuries later by playwright William Shakespeare.

1043–99 Life of Spanish hero Rodrigo Díaz de Vivar (El Cid) a major figure in the Reconquista of Muslim Spain by Christian kingdoms.

1046 Before his coronation, Henry III of the Holy Roman Empire imposes his own candidate for the papacy, launching 200 years of struggle between the Vatican and the Holy Roman Emperors.

◀ **Pope Gregory VII.**

Statue of El Cid in Burgos, Spain. ▼

1066 William the Conquerer leads Norman Conquest of England. He introduces the feudal system and remains duke of Normandy in France.

1071 Battle of Manzikert. Seljuq Turks, who have migrated from the east and are attempting to settle in Anatolia, defeat the Byzantines, who lose their Asian provinces.

1070 Saint Margaret of Scotland (c.1045–1093) marries Malcolm III of Scotland. She brings the Scottish church into line with that of Rome, and from then on Iona becomes less influential in religious affairs.

c.1075 Pope Gregory VII introduces the Gregorian Reforms, aiming to strengthen the Papal position over secular rulers. He confirms the requirement of clerical celibacy and launches the Investiture Controversy, a contest about whether the church or monarchs can appoint officials such as bishops and abbots.

RELIGION

1040–1105 Life of Rashi (Shlomo Yitzhaki) of Tours, France, who writes comprehensive commentaries on the Jewish Talmud and Tanakh.

1042 Edward the Confessor builds Westminster Abbey in London.

1054 The Great Schism: the Roman Catholic church and the eastern patriarchies formally break away from each other.

SCIENCE AND LEARNING

1033–1109 Life of Burgundian philosopher St. Anselm of Canterbury.

1046 The popes begin to reform the Catholic church.

1059 As part of the papal reformation, cardinals rather than secular leaders are given the sole right of electing new popes.

c.1050 New agricultural equipment such as crop rotation and the application of heavy plows help to improve the economy.

1150s onward Hospitals and universities that are separate from church institutes begin to appear all over Europe.

1078 The cathedral of Santiago de Compostela is built in Spain. It becomes the major pilgrimage center in Europe.

TRADE AND EXPLORATION

Tournai Cathedral, built in 1066. ▶

A scene showing Edward the Confessor on the Bayeux Tapestry. ▶

THE ARTS

1063 St. Mark's Basilica, Venice is begun.

1066 Work begins on Tournai Cathedral, France, incorporating Gothic and Romanesque elements. ✱ Bayeaux Tapestry depicting Norman conquest of England is woven.

1077 Hohensalzburg Castle in Austria is begun.

SOCIETY AND EVERYDAY LIFE

▲ **The east face of Westminster Abbey.**

A bailiff directing peasants at work in the fields. ▶

HIGH MIDDLE AGES

1086 Almoravid dynasty of Muslim Berbers from north Africa take over Spain.

A golden shell, the emblem of St. James, marking the Pilgrims' Way to Santiago Cathedral. ▼

1084 The Carthusian order of monks is founded. The name derives from the Chartreuse Mountains where the founder, St. Bruno, establishes his first monastery. The word "Charterhouse" also derives from this.

1087 The relics of St. Nicholas of Myra in Turkey, one of the founder myths of Santa Claus, are stolen away and housed in a new church of St. Nicholas at Bari, Italy.

1086 The Domesday Book is completed in England, a record of landowners.

Hildegard of Bingen. ▼

1088 University of Bologna, Italy is the first formal university, originally teaching just law.

c.1083 The *Carmen Campidoctoris* (*Song of the Campeador*) is composed in Spain about the hero El Cid.

◄ **Knights would ensure that their heraldic emblems were visible on their horses, as well as on their own surcoats.**

1080 The medical school at Salerno, Italy offers 5-year courses.

late 11th century The couched lance, which is held under a knight's arm, is developed.

1095 Pope Urban II calls for the first Crusade to reclaim the Holy Land from Muslims.

1096 On their way to the Holy Land, Crusaders massacre Jews living along the Rhine river in Germany.

1097–9 First Crusade. Christians capture Jerusalem, massacre much of the Muslim and Jewish population, and establish the Kingdom of Jerusalem along with other crusader states: the County of Tripoli, the County of Edessa, and the Principality of Antioch.

◄ **Crusader knights receive the blessing of the pope.**

1098 The Cistercian or Trappist monastic order is founded by St. Bernard of Clairvaux, with all monasteries dedicated to Mary, Mother of God. This is the first time a woman is given central significance in the Christian religion.

1098–1179 Life of German abbess, poet and medical writer Hildegard of Bingen.

11th century Stone churches begin to replace simple local wooden churches.

1100 The Carthusian monastic order is founded.

1100–60 Life of Italian theologian Christian Lombard.

1093 Construction of Durham Cathedral, north England begins, including stone rib vaulting for the first time in a cathedral.

◄ **An illustration from *The Song of Roland*.**

11th century Troubadours, musical poets exposing chivalry and courtly love, appear in southern France and spread around southern Europe. In northern France they are known as trouvères.

1097 The wooden castle structures with timber palisades begin to be replaced with stone buildings, such as the White Tower at the Tower of London.

c.1098–1100 *The Song of Roland* is written by an unknown French author about the massacre of Charlemagne's rearguard at Roncesvalles.

1096 Crusaders returning from the Middle East introduce new diseases such as leprosy.

1100 Many Germans (including Jews) migrate to Poland in search of a better life.

1108 With the reign of Louis VI, advised by Abbot Suger, the kings of the Franks gain more and more authority over other nobles in France.

St. Bernard of Clairvaux. ▼

◄ **Krak des Chevaliers in Syria, one of the most important Crusader castles built in the Middle East.**

◄ **The Tower of London as it is today at night.**

late 11th century William the Conqueror and later Norman kings build more defensive castles all around England, including Windsor Castle and the Tower of London.

HIGH MIDDLE AGES

POLITICS, DYNASTIES, AND WARS

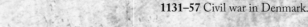

1131–57 Civil war in Denmark.

1123 German princes abolish hereditary kingship and establish the right to elect German kings.

1139 With victory over the Muslims at the battle of Ourique, part of the Iberian peninsula becomes the separate Christian kingdom of Portugal.

1139–53 Civil war in England between Stephen and Matilda.

◄ **Although the knightly order became wealthy, the Templar knights themselves gave all their riches to the order, so as individuals they were poor. Their poverty is symbolized by having to share a horse.**

◄ **Edinburgh Castle, Scotland, built in 1130, overlooks the city. Monarchs and great lords created strongholds such as these to reinforce their control of a city or region.**

RELIGION

1113 The Knights Hospitaller gain papal recognition as a monastic order.

1115 Clairvaux Monastery in France is founded under St. Bernard.

1119 The Knights Templar order is formed.

1122 Treaty of Metz/Concordat of Worms. In settlement of the Investiture Conflict, when secular and papal authorities argue about who can appoint religious officials, Holy Roman Emperor Henry V and Pope Callistus II agree that the church can invest clergy with religious authority, but the king would give them political authority and ownership of lands.

1123 First Lateran Council held in Rome to discuss religious law.

SCIENCE AND LEARNING

1114–87 Life of Gerard of Cremona, an Italian scholar who goes to Muslim Spain to study and translate Greek, Jewish, and Arabic works.

1116 The astronomical tables produced by the Arab mathematician al-Battani are translated into Latin.

A Gothic rose window, this one from Chartres. ▼

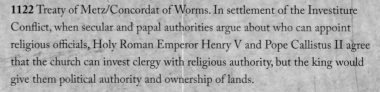

TRADE AND EXPLORATION

▲ **The** *stave* **church at Borgund, Norway, built around 1180.**

THE ARTS

▲ **Windsor Castle in England has been continually occupied for longer than any other castle in Europe.** >>

mid-12th century Wooden *stave* churches, probably modelled on pagan temples, are built across Norway.

1130–44 Designing the present-day Basilica of Saint Denis in Paris, the first true European cathedral, Abbot Suger develops the Gothic style of architecture, including the first rose windows.

1122 A hillfort at Alcazar, Spain, is the forerunner of the later castle.

1132 Fountains Abbey in north England is founded.

SOCIETY AND EVERYDAY LIFE

1121 The philosopher Peter Abelard (1079–1142) is castrated because of his affair with Hélöise.

1131 Most of the world's Jewish population now lives in Spain.

▲ **A leper holding the bell they had to ring to warn uninfected people that they were approaching.**

1123 St. Bartholomew's Hospital is founded in London, England.

◄ **A later painting showing Abelard and Hélöise parting.**

1145–9 Second Crusade. Europeans soundly defeated by Saracens but en route to the Holy Land an English force helps the Portuguese defeat Muslims at Lisbon.

1151 The extremist Berber dynasty the Almohads take over Muslim Spain. Jews and Christians begin to leave.

1157 Waldemar the Great makes Denmark a great nation.

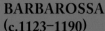

◄ **Emperor Friedrich Barbarossa.**

1167 England invades Ireland and Anglo-Normans begin to interfere in Irish affairs.

1154–89 Rule of Henry II of England, first of the Plantagenet dynasty, who strengthens the monarchy, creates an efficient government and bureaucracy, and makes England a powerful kingdom.

1154 Holy Roman Emperor Friedrich Barbarossa begins his campaigns against the Normans in Sicily, conquering several states in Italy.

BARBAROSSA (c.1123–1190)

Nicknamed Barbarossa (Italian for "Redbeard") because of his coloring, Friedrich or Frederick was the son of Frederick II, duke of Swabia. He became Frederick III of Swabia in 1147, then in 1152 he was elected king of the Germans and was crowned Holy Roman emperor Frederick I in 1155.

A handsome, charismatic, capable and famous leader, Frederick aimed to strengthen the position of the Empire nationally and internationally. In imposing law across the vast imperial territories, he became a symbol of a strong, unified Germany.

His expeditions to assert control over the wealthy northern Italian city-states had little success. Also, his clashes with several popes led to a period of excommunication. His did strengthen the German crown, although after his death the area reverted to a series of territorial states.

He drowned en route to the Third Crusade, but in German legend he is only sleeping, and will awaken when the country needs him.

◄ **A painting of Henry II of England from the effigy on his tomb.**

c.1155 Peter Lombard writes the *Book of Sentences* that becomes a standard text giving answers to theological questions.

c.1150 University of Paris founded.

◄ **Troubadours paying court to their queen.**

1158 English scientist Robert Grosseteste (c.1170–1253) works on optics, astronomy and mathematics. He also translates Aristotle's *Ethics*.

1167 University of Oxford founded in England.

c.1159–72 Life of Benjamin of Tudela, who travels from Spain around North Africa and writes important account of the Jewish communities he visits.

◄ **The soldier is blue is wearing a chainmail coif.**

Rothenburg ob der Tauber in Bavaria, Germany is a well-preserved medieval town, one of many that grew and flourished during this period. ▼

1150s Queen Eleanor of Aquitaine (married to Henry II of England) sees her court at Poitiers, France become a center of artistic culture and poetry.

c.1150 German poets, influenced by the Provençal and French troubadours, develop courtly love songs. They become known as minnesingers.

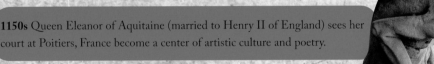

◄ **A gargoyle on Notre Dame Cathedral, Paris**

1144 First Blood Libel: in Norwich, England, Jews are accused of killing Christian children for religious ceremonies.

1147–1219 Life of the English knight William Marshal.

1150 After the Berber Almohad occupation of Spain, many Jews flee to North Africa or the Middle East.

1100s The fitted headdress the coif is introduced.

1159 The town of Lübeck is founded on the Baltic coast.

HIGH MIDDLE AGES

POLITICS, DYNASTIES, AND WARS

1170 Supported by their mother Eleanor of Aquitaine, the sons of Henry II of England (Richard the Lionheart, John, and Geoffrey) rebel against him. ❀ Stefan Nemanja founds the first Serbian kingdom.

▲ **Richard the Lionheart.**

◄The murder of Thomas à Becket.

Clifford's Tower, York, site of a massacre of Jews. ▼

1187 The Kurdish/Turkish Islamic general Saladin captures the city of Jerusalem from the Christian kingdom.

1189–99 Rule of Richard I, the Lionheart in England. He spends only a total of 6 months in the country.

1189–92 Third Crusade (King's Crusade). Led by Richard the Lionheart and Philip II of France, Crusaders win some victories but fail in their main aim of reclaiming Jerusalem. Richard and Saladin agree a treaty allowing unarmed Christian pilgrims and merchants to visit Jerusalem.

1190 Massacre of about 150 Jews in York, England.

12th century Vienna becomes the capital of Austria.

1170 Archbishop Thomas à Becket is murdered in Canterbury Cathedral, England. He is canonised 3 years later.

1173 Bernard of Clairvaux canonized.

1174 French merchant Peter Valdes founds the Waldensian sect.

1100s Dynastic struggle between the Guelphs and the Ghibellines in Italy/Holy Roman Empire.

RELIGION

1177 Treaty of Venice. Holy Roman Emperor Friedrich Barbarossa and Pope Alexander III unite to combat heretics as both secular and religious enemies.

1179 Third Lateran Council decides that only cardinals can elect popes, and condemns Waldensian and Albigensian heresies.

1184 Excommunication of the Gnostic sects the Cathars and Waldensians, mainly based in southern France.

1194–1253 Life of Clare of Assisi (Clair or Claire) or Chiara Offreduccio, follower of Francis of Assisi. She founds the Order of Poor Ladies, commonly known as the Poor Clares, the first monastic rule for women.

SCIENCE AND LEARNING

◄Walther von der Vogelweide.

12th century The siege engine the trebuchet is developed.

▼ Bojnice Castle still contains some 12th-century elements.

TRADE AND EXPLORATION

▲ **Chartres Cathedral is a perfect example of Gothic architecture.**

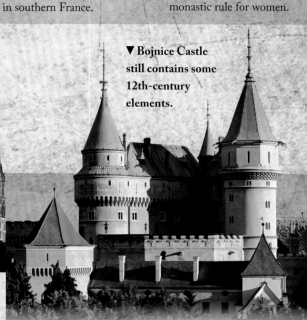

▲ **The Leaning Tower of Pisa, begun in 1174.**

THE ARTS

c.1170–1220 Life of German minnesinger Wolfram von Eschenbach.

c.1170–1230 Life of Walther von der Vogelweide, considered to be the greatest of the German minnesingers.

1174 Construction starts on the campanile or bell tower of Pisa Cathedral – the Leaning Tower of Pisa.

1183 The *Primary Chronicle of Rus* is compiled, outlining the history of the Rus Vikings who rule from Kiev in Russia and eventually lead to Tsarist Russia.

12th century Spis Castle in Slovakia is built. ❀ The original Bojnice Castle in Slovakia is built.

c.1190 German musical love poets (minnesänger/minnesingers) develop their own lyrical form.

1193 Work begins on Chartres Cathedral, France, a shining example of Gothic architecture and of medieval cathedrals.

SOCIETY AND EVERYDAY LIFE

◄The longbow and the crossbow in action.

12th century Agricultural developments – particularly the cultivation of beans – mean that for the first time there is plenty of food for every class of society, and the population begins to grow. ❀ Towns, trade and merchants, travel and communication all expand, Gothic art develops and western Europe becomes more powerful. These changes lay the foundations of the Renaissance and the modern world. ❀ The longbow is developed from the shorter hunting bows. Using it, a skilled archer can kill an enemy 400 yards/366 meters away. Even so, the more powerful crossbow begins to take over.

HIGH MIDDLE AGES

1202 Philip II of France defeats John of England, taking most of England's French possessions. His demonstration of strength gives him a firm rule over French lords. ✥ Fourth Crusade launched. In 1204, forces of the Crusade are persuaded by Venice to sack Constantinople and establish a new Latin monarchy there.

1204 Alexios Komnenos of Byzantium captures the city of Trebizon and the province of Chaldia, on the Black Sea coast. Although only a small kingdom it is grandly called the Empire of Trebizond, and later becomes a vassal kingdom of Byzantium.

1209–29 Crusade against Albigensian heretics in southern France.

◀ **Most children who tried to reach the Holy Land ended up dead or enslaved.**

1212 Grenada is now the only major Muslim state in Spain.

1215 Magna Carta. The barons of England force King John to sign this early charter of rights.

▲ **King John signs the Magna Carta.**

1199 Pope Innocent III founds the Inquisition to seek out heresy.

1209 St. Francis of Assisi (c.1182–1226) founds the Franciscan order that embraces poverty as an imitation of the life of Christ.

◀ **St. Francis of Assisi praying with another Franciscan monk.**

1212 The disastrous Children's Crusade.

1215 Fourth Lateran Council accepts the doctrine of transubstantiation, believing that the flesh and blood of Christ is manifest in the consecrated Host and wine. The council decides that Jews must wear special badges.

1216 The Dominican order of friars is founded by St. Dominic of Spain to end heresy and to convert Jews and Muslims. Many members of the later inquisitions are Dominicans.

c.1200 Lay education begins, when students enter schools and universities without intending to become priests. Latin begins to lose its grip over learning, the Church begins to lose control over knowledge, and cathedral schools become general universities.

1202 Leonardo Fibonacci of Italy (1170–1250) introduces the Arab-Hindu numerical system to Europe in his book *Liber Abaci* (*The Book of the Abacus*).

c.1206–80 Life of German philosopher St. Albert the Great (Albertus Magnus).

1209 University of Cambridge founded in England.

◀ **Fibonacci**

▲ **Albertus Magnus**

c.1214–c.1292 Life of English scientist Roger Bacon.

St. John's College, Cambridge University today. ▶

1197 Chateau Galliard or Saucy Castle is built by Richard the Lionheart near Rouen, France.

1202 Death of Igor Svyatoslavich in the Don Valley, who is immortalized in the Slavic epic *The Tale of Igor's Campaign.*

1206–78 Life of Italian sculptor and architect Nicola Pisano.

early 1200s Castle construction becomes more scientific, with concentric fortifications, many defensive towers, and often a polygonal shape.

1210 When Pope Innocent III bans clergy from acting on the stage in public, mystery plays are run by town guilds, who introduce comic elements and perform in the vernacular rather than in Latin.

▲ **The fortified town of Carcassonne, restored in the 19th century, was a stronghold of the Albigensians or Cathars.**

1200 By now tournaments have settled into spectator sports with formal jousting, team fights, and archery competitions.

c.1200 Pointed shoes begin to appear.

1200–78 Life of the Austrian knight Ulrich von Liechtenstein who wears a famous helmet featuring the Roman goddess of love, Venus.

◀ **Long, pointed shoes became highly fashionable.**

1215 The Fourth Lateran Council decides that Jews and Muslims have to wear distinguishing clothes, such as special hats or yellow ring-badges for Jews, and crescent badges for Muslims.

by 1200 The wimple is introduced for women, a headdress under the headveil that wraps around the neck and sometimes the chin.

POLITICS, DYNASTIES, AND WARS

1223 Mongols first attack Russia (Kievan Rus). Louis VIII of France begins to conquer southern France.

1225 Teutonic Knights embark on a crusade in Prussia and further east, ruling lands that they conquer/convert.

1226–70 Reign of Louis IX of France (St. Louis). The most powerful ruler in Europe, he is widely respected as a Christian prince (he goes on Crusade) and a just and saintly man. His rule is considered to be "the golden century of St. Louis."

▲ **Knights of the Teutonic Order.**

1231 Teutonic Knights take Prussia.

1230s The term "parliament" is first used for the Great Council in England that advises the kings.

1237–42 Mongols of the Golden Horde invade Europe. Called Tatars by the Russians, they sack Kiev in 1240, defeat a Polish army as they pass through Poland, devastate Hungary in 1241, and reach into Austria. They only withdraw on the death of the Great Khan, to take part in the election of the next emperor, but remain in control of Russia.

The Inquisition prepares to burn heretics to death. ▶

1232 Pope Gregory IX creates the Papal Inquisition.

RELIGION

1224 Order of the Teutonic Knights is founded to crusade against the pagans of northern Europe.

1233 Jewish authorities in Montpelier, France burn the works of the Spanish Jewish philosopher Maimonides (1134–1204).

1235–1350 Life of Majorcan philosopher and alchemist Ramon Lull.

1236–1305 Life of French Jewish astronomer Jacob ben Machir ibn Tibbon who invents an improved astrolabe.

SCIENCE AND LEARNING

c.1225–74 Life of Italian philosopher St. Thomas Aquinas, the most influential thinker in the Scholastic tradition.

Ramon (Raymond) Lull, 13th-century philosopher and alchemist/scientist. ▶

◀ **Marriage of St. Louis IX of France to Margaret, daughter of Raymond Beranger, Count of Provence. Their descendants rule France until the French Revolution.**

TRADE AND EXPLORATION

13th and 14th centuries As the Mongol Empire controls and defends most of the Silk Road, transport of the precious silk is facilitated to the west.

Part of the Silk Road today. Passing through wasteland and desert, risking bandit attacks and starvation en route, the rewards for merchants who successfully transported goods along the Road were enormous. ▼

1230 Work begins on the Basilica di San Francesco in Assisi, Italy. Work begins on York Minster in northern England – a minster is a cathedral which undertakes missionary work..

THE ARTS

1230–1298 Life of Jacobus de Varagine, archbishop of Genoa, Italy, who compiles the popular book *Golden Legends* (*Legenda Aurea*) about the lives of saints.

c.1230 The first part of the French love poem *The Romance of the Rose* is written.

1236 The Great Mosque in Cordoba, Spain is converted into a cathedral.

1221 Burgos Cathedral in Spain is begun.

SOCIETY AND EVERYDAY LIFE

c.1220 Legend of the Wandering Jew first appears in Italy.

1200s A castle is added to the stern and bow of north European ships.

1226–70 Louis IX of France (St. Louis) develops a uniform code of law for the whole country.

mid 13th century The long-handled bill weapon is developed for foot soldiers, with a curving bill and a spike.

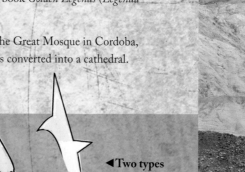

◀ **Two types of bill.**

1240 Alexander Nevsky of the Russian city-state Novgorod defeats Sweden and the Teutonic Knights. He is a vassal of the Mongols.

1241 Poland divides into 4 separate states.

1242 Bohemia takes control of Austria.

1244 Turks destroy the final remnants of the Christian kingdom of Jerusalem.

1249 Portuguese recapture Faro on the southern coast from Muslims and complete the Renconquista of Portugal.

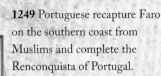

◄ **Knights embarking on military expeditions displayed their heraldic emblems on the ships.**

1243 About 12,000 copies of the Jewish Talmud are burnt in Paris.

1250 Successors of Pope Innocent III are involved in a political struggle with Frederick II of the Holy Roman Empire, who attempts to take control in central Italy. They order a crusade against him, the first time a crusade is called for political reasons. The popes are championed by Charles of Anjou, from the French royal line, who defeats Frederick's heirs and wins Sicily.

1256–83 Under Llewellyn ap Gruffydd, the Welsh rebel against English rule but are eventually defeated.

1256 Lengthy war begins between Venice and Genoa

1259 Mongols from the Golden Horde raid Polish and Lithuanian cities. They later raid Byzantine territories and Bulgaria, but are defeated in Hungary by a reformed army.

1256 Order of Augustinian friars established.

1261 Byzantine Emperor Michael VIII Paliologos recaptures Constantinople after 60 years of foreign occupation. Alexios Strategopoulos, Michael's general, leads a small force into the city through a secret passage in the Theodosian Wall. However the city's wealth has been plundered and Byzantium never recovers.

1263 Barons' War in England, when Simon de Montfort rebels against Henry III and is defeated at the Battle of Evesham. ✇ Scotland defeats Norway at the battle of Largs for control of the Western Isles, although the Lords of the Isles remain semi-independent for 200 years.

Cologne Cathedral, built in 1248. ►

1240s The botanical encyclopedia of the Spanish Arab Ibn al-Baitar is translated into Latin and soon becomes a standard textbook.

c.1252–70 Based on the work of the Spanish Arab al-Zarqali, the astronomical *Alfonsine Tables* are produced.

◄ **A European view of the Coronation of the Great Khan of the Mongols.**

1241 The hansa or trading guilds of the towns of Lübeck and Hamburg form an alliance, the precursor of the later Hanseatic League.

1259–66 Niccolo and Maffeo Polo (father and uncle of Marco) are the first Europeans known to travel the length of the Silk Road from Europe to China ("Cathay"), where they meet China's Mongol emperor.'

c.1260–c.1327 Life of German philosopher and theologian Meister (Master) Eckhart.

c.1266–1308 Life of Scottish/Irish philosopher John Duns Scotus.

Women admirers surround a knight. ►

c.1240–1302 Life of Italian artist Cimabue.

1248 Cologne Cathedral in Germany is built.

1250–1314 Life of architect and sculptor Giovanni Pisano, son of Nicola.

1266/67 or 1276–1337 Life of the Italian painter Giotto.

◄ Heroic knights and exciting tournaments were a feature of medieval life in "The Age of Chivalry." ►

c.1250 There is a "Little Ice Age" of overall colder temperatures until about 1850.

◄ **Philip IV of France.**

1278 Under Rudolph I, the Habsburg dynasty of the Holy Roman Empire takes control of Austria.

1280 Russian vassals of Mongols move their headquarters to Moscow.

1282–1302 Vespers War in Sicily. Sicilians revolt against unpopular French Angevin rule.

1283 With the defeat of Llewellyn, Prince of Wales, Edward I of England completes conquest of Wales.

1284 Battle of Meloria. Genoa defeats Pisa and takes control of Corsica.

1285–1314 Reign of Philip IV of France (le Bel or the Fair), who strengthens the legal bureaucracy, appoints popes, and destroys the Knights Templar.

1291 Swiss cantons set up Eternal Union for protection against other states.

1292 John Balliol becomes king in Scotland after Scottish nobles ask Edward I of England to adjudicate in order to prevent civil war between rival claimants.

1295 The "Auld Alliance" is formed between Scotland and France.

1296–8 War between England and Scotland. Edward I of England, "Hammer of the Scots", sends an invasion force that deposes King John, but is defeated by William Wallace and Andrew de Moray the following year. Edward defeats the Scots in 1298 but cannot hold Scotland.

1298 Battle of Curzola. Genoa defeats Venice. ❀ Massacres of Jews in Germany.

◄ **A page from a breviary belonging to Philip IV of France.**

13th century The chronicler Martin of Opava introduces the legend of a female pope, Pope Joan.

▲ **Santa Maria del Fiore, Florence**

1270 Venetian glass-makers develop spectacles.

1279 The work of Iranian doctor Rhazes is translated into Latin as *The Comprehensive Book*, and becomes a standard medical textbook for centuries.

c.1287–1347 Life of English philosopher William of Ockham, who uses the principle of simplicity known as Occam's Razor.

13th century Public Turkish baths introduced by Crusaders.

▼ **Malbork Castle.**

Marco Polo. ▶

1275–92 Marco Polo (1254–1324), one of a group of Italian merchants, visits China and takes service under emperor Kublai Khan. His memoirs provide a lasting account of Chinese culture and inspire explorers to find new routes to the fabled lands of the East.

1274 The Teutonic Knights build Malbork Castle in Poland.

1280 Muiden Castle in the Netherlands is built.

1283 Caernarvon Castle in Wales is built.

1296 Work begins on the cathedral of Santa Maria del Fiore, Florence.

◄ **Detail of a suit of plate armor.**

13th century The oldest surviving versions of the Nibelungenleid are written down in Middle High-German. This records the much older story of the dragon-slayer Siegfried.

1275 Plate mail is developed.

1290 Jews expelled from England.

Bathing in the 13th century. ▶

13th century The halbard is developed, a weapon with an axe blade and a spike. ❀ The first sumptuary laws appear, determining which social classes may wear certain colors and materials. ❀ Medieval civilization is at its height with the arts, Scholastic philosophy, and civil society all flourishing.

late 13th century Tunics become tighter fitting instead of the previous loose fit. ❀ The longsword is developed.

1305 During Scottish war of independence against England, Scottish leader William Wallace is captured and executed.

1309 The Knights of St. John set up base in Rhodes.

The Fort of St. Nicholas, Rhodes, begun in 1309. ▼

1310 The city of Venice in Italy forms a ruling Council of Ten.

1312 Templar Knights destroyed at the urging of Philip IV of France. ✸ Lyons becomes part of France.

1314 Scottish leader Robert the Bruce wins battle of Bannockburn against England and secures Scottish independence. ✸ Jacques de Molay, Grand Master of the Templars, is burnt at the stake in Paris for heresy. Other Templars are also executed.

1315 Battle of Mortgarten. Swiss defeat Austrian Habsburg invasion.

1317 France adopts the Salic Law barring women from succeeding to the throne.

1314 For more than two years no pope is elected.

1302 Pope Boniface II defends the principle of papal jurisdiction over all creatures in *Unam Sanctam*.

1303–73 Life of St. Bridget of Sweden who founds the Bridgettine order of nuns and monks.

1309 The Popes are based at Avignon, France instead of at Rome. For most of the century, France controls the papacy and most cardinals and popes are French.

▲ **A medieval view of the Pope speaking in council.**

1316 The Italian doctor Mondino (c.1270–1326) writes *Anathomia*, the first "modern" textbook on anatomy.

1302 The first known judicial post-mortem in Europe is carried out in Bologna, Italy.

1304 The French surgeon Henri de Mondeville (c.1260–1320) teaches anatomy at Montpellier. He advocates hygiene when treating wounds.

▼ **A Gothic-style painting by Simone Martini of Siena, Italy (1280–1344) of the Madonna with saints.**

▲ **Scenes from a medieval manuscript on medicine.**

▲ **Templars burning at the stake.**

1300 The International Gothic style of painting and decorative arts develops, with color and pattern dominating. ✸ Most of Reims Cathedral, where French monarchs are crowned, is completed.

1307 Hunyad Castle in Transylvania (present-day Romania) is built.

1308–21 The Italian playwright Dante Alighieri (1265–1321) writes the *Divine Comedy.*

1314 *Roman de Fauvel* (*The Story of the Fawn-Colored Beast*) is published by French poet Gervais du Bus.

1300 By now European courts are fashion-conscious and follow trends slavishly.

1306 Jews expelled from France.

◄ **Dante Alighieri**

early 14th century Gunpowder is introduced and early cannons are used.

1315 Widespread famine in northwestern Europe follows crop failure due to bad weather.

▲ **With civil society functioning again projects such as road construction take place.**

1323–25 Pisa and Genoa war over control of Sardinia and Corsica.

1328 The House of Valois claims the French throne under Philip VI.

1333–70 Kazimierz III Wielki (Casimir the Great) rules Poland, bringing an era of cultural and political unity, with the capital at Krakow.

1337 Hundred Years' War between England and France begins.

1338 Treaty of Koblenz between England and the Holy Roman Empire.

1343 The Spanish kingdom of Aragon seizes Majorca.

1347 Serbs occupy Albania.

▼ **The Battle of Crécy in the Hundred Years' War**

St. Catherine of Siena. ▶

1342–1413 Life of female English mystic, Julian of Norwich.

1347–80 Life of the theologian and philosopher St. Catherine of Siena, along with St. Francis of Assisi one of the patron saints of Italy.

1330s Petrarch, the Italian poet, scholar, and humanist Francesco Petrarca (1304–74) first uses the term "Dark Ages" to apply to the early Middle Ages when there was a scarcity of Latin texts to study.

▲ **Chaucer shown in a 14th century manuscript on horseback as his pilgrims riding to Canterbury are often depicted.**

▼ **The Palace of the Popes at Avignon.**

1325 The Moorish Arab explorer ibn Battuta (1304–68/9) travels more than 75,000 miles through southern and eastern Europe as well as Africa and the Far East. His report is widely available in Europe.

▲ **Later Medieval ships with their square sails and 'castles' raised above deck level.**

▲ **The eastern "Gates of Paradise" of the Florence baptistery.**

1334 Work begins on the Palace of the Popes, Avignon.

1336 Andrea Pisano (1295–1348) creates the bronze south doors for the baptistery of Florence.

c.1343–1400 Life of English poet Geoffrey Chaucer, who writes *The Canterbury Tales*.

1348 The Italian Giovanni Boccaccio (1313–75) begins to write the stories of the *Decameron*, the first prose narrative. ✱ Construction begins on Karlstejn Castle, in Bohemia, now the Czech Republic. ✱ The troubadours disappear around the time of the Black Death.

During plague epidemics flagellants thought that they could appease the wrath of God by mortifying their bodies. ▶

1340 The population of Europe is about 70 million.

1348 Order of the Garter founded in England.

1348–51 Black Death: bubonic plague devastates Europe, killing at least a third of the population. Further plagues follow.

LATE MIDDLE AGES

1353 Swiss Confederation founded.

1356 English win the battle of Poitiers during the Hundred Years' War. 🌑 Holy Roman Emperor Charles IV issues the Golden Bull, which declares that elections of the emperor will not depend upon the Pope.

1360–90s Ottoman Turks conquer Greece, Thrace, and Bulgaria.

1361–70 Hanseatic League war against Denmark. The League wins a trade monopoly in Scandinavia.

1373 John of Gaunt leads new English invasion of France.

1378 Florentine ciompi or wool-carders take over government for a brief period.

A detail of the intricate work that covers the Alhambra palace.▶

1358 French Jacquerie peasant revolt is suppressed by nobles.

▲ The first folio of the Golden Bull.

Karlstejn Castle in the Czech Republic, begun in 1348. ▶

1378–1417 Great Western Schism of the popes begins with the election of two popes: Urban VI who stays in Rome, and Clement VII, who sets up court in Avignon, France.

1350 Ship-building improves by combining carvel planking (edge to edge planks) with stern and bow castles, a square sail to give power, and a lanteen sail for maneuverability. These make possible the later voyages of discovery.

1357 The book *The Travels of Sir John Mandeville* is first published. An account of the Middle East, parts of Africa and the Far East, it becomes popular in many countries, although the author is mainly sensationalizing the writings of earlier travelers.

1358 The Hanseatic League is founded. Also known as the Hanse or Hansa, it is an alliance of trading cities and merchant guilds that comes to dominate trade in northern Europe.

◀ The city walls of Talinn in Estonia, a Hanse stronghold.

Bran Castle today. ▶

c. 1350 The old oral stories of the Welsh *Mabinogion* are written down in *The White Book of Rhydderch*.

Late Middle Ages Most artists are now laymen, and their work is often commissioned by wealthy individuals for their personal enjoyment.

c.1360–87 The poem *Piers Plowman* is written in Middle English by William Langland.

1362 The Alhambra palace complex is built at Grenada, Spain.

1363–c.1430 Life of Venetian-born poet Christine de Pizan, the first professional female writer in Europe.

1369 French historian Jean Froissart begins to write his Chronicles, covering 1322 to 1400.

c.1377 Bran Castle in Romania, associated with the Dracula legend, is finished. Construction is begun by the Teutonic Knights.

c.1350 Parti-colored or *mi-parti* clothes are introduced, with each piece made of two different colors or fabrics. In particular, the legs of hose would be different colors.

Late Middle Ages Castles are now not only defensive positions, but sophisticated emblems of a lord's wealth and status.

1364 Casimir the Great gives Jews rights in Poland, and Jewish settlement there grows.

1377–99 Reign of Richard II of England, who might have invented the handkerchief.

Prague Castle dominates the skyline of the city, as an example of how the nobles' power is expressed in their buildings. ▶

LATE MIDDLE AGES

POLITICS, DYNASTIES, AND WARS

1380 Dimitri Donskoi of Moscow leads Russian principalities to victory over the Mongols at Kulikovo.

1381 Peasants' Revolt in England.

1384 The northern part of modern Belgium known as Flanders, including the wealthy, urbane cities of Bruges, Ghent, and Ypres, comes under the domain of Burgundy.

1385 Battle of Aljubarrota. John I wins the Portuguese throne from Castile.

1386 Battle of Sempach. Swiss again defeat Austria. Poland and Lithuania unite through marriage, creating one of the largest polities in Europe. England and Portugal agree the Treaty of Windsor, creating long-standing alliance.

1388 Supported by Margarethe, queen of Denmark and Norway, Swedish nobles rise up against their unpopular king, Albert.

1389 Battle of Kosovo. Ottoman Turks defeat Serbs, and take Serbia and Bosnia. They now effectively rule the Balkans.

1396 Battle of Nicopolis. A Christian crusade to stop the Turkish advance in eastern Europe is crushed by the Ottomans, who go on to take more of the Byzantine Empire, leaving it with just a few provinces in Greece and the city of Constantinople.

1397 Kalmar Union. Denmark, Norway and Sweden become a single country united by Margaret (Margaretha) I of Denmark.

1391 Forced conversions of Jews and Moors in Aragon, Spain.

◄ **Margarethe I of Denmark and Norway.**

RELIGION

1382–4 The church reformer John Wycliffe (c.1328–1384) translates the Bible into English. He is posthumously declared a heretic, but his followers, the Lollards, continue to protest against corruption.

SCIENCE AND LEARNING

14th century The term "Middle Ages" is first used to indicate the gap between the Classical period and the resurgence of scholarship in the Renaissance.

TRADE AND EXPLORATION

◄ **A page from John Wycliffe's Bible.**

St. Lawrence receiving the Treasures of the Church, by Fra Angelico. ▶

THE ARTS

1382 The oldest known document in Yiddish, the Cambridge Yiddish Codex.

c.1382 *The Red Book of Hergest* records oral Welsh stories that compose the *Mabinogion*.

14th century As the power of the church declines, music becomes more secular and is centered around courts.

1386 Work begins on Milan Cathedral in Italy, one of the largest Gothic buildings.

1390–1441 Life of Flemish painter Jan van Eyck.

1395–1455 Life of Italian artist Fra Angelico.

1397–1450 Life of Italian painter Pisano.

SOCIETY AND EVERYDAY LIFE

c.1380 The *houpeland* robe, with a high collar and very full, trailing sleeves appears. This evolves into modern academic robes.

14th century Long, pointed shoes now become extremely exaggerated.

1393 The Bal des Ardents in Paris, France (Ball of the Burning Men) is typical of the grand fancy-dress parties indulged in by the rich and powerful. King Charles VI and other lords dress up as "wild men" tied as a group in shaggy costumes held together by pitch or wax. When one man catches fire from a torch, the conflagration kills 4 and injures several people.

1394 Jews expelled from France again.

1400–09 Owen Glendower's Welsh rebellion against English rule ends in failure.

1403 Battle of Shrewsbury in England. Henry IV defeats Harry "Hotspur" Percy.

1399 In England, Richard II is deposed by Henry IV.

1407 Civil war breaks out in France after Louis, Duke of Orleans is murdered by Burgundians.

1407–56 Life of John Hunyadi of Hungary, who fought against the Ottoman Empire.

1410 Battle of Tannenberg. Teutonic Knights defeated by Poles and Lithuanians and begin to decline.

1411 Sigismund, King of Hungary is elected German King and crowned Holy Roman Emperor.

1415 England wins battle of Agincourt in France.

1419 Defenestration of Prague. Reformist followers of the executed Jan Hus break into Prague town hall and throw Catholic councillors out of the windows. ❀ Sigismund takes Bohemia.

1419–34 Hussite War in Bohemia (now Czech Republic). Followers of the reformer Jan Hus rebel against the Holy Roman Emperor.

early 1400s Led by Cosimo de Medici (1389–1464), the wealthy banking family the Medicis begin to dominate Florence.

1409 Venice expands its area of influence into Dalmatia and Lombardy.

◄ **Coronation of Henry IV, Westminster, England, from Froissart's Chronicles.**

1414–1417 Great Western Schism of popes ends with the Council of Constance, the largest medieval church meeting. The Council decides to replace all three rival popes with the election of Pope Martin V. The Council also excommunicates Jan Hus.

1400 The Czech reformer Jan Hus (John Huss) is ordained a priest. He goes on to condemn church corruption and support Wycliffe's anticlericalism.

1408 In England, it becomes illegal to translate the Bible into English or read it in English without the permission of a bishop.

6 July, 1415 Jan Hus is burned to death for heresy in Constance, Switzerland.

1409 With the election of Alexander V there are now three popes.

◄ **A memorial to Jan Hus in the Czech Republic.**

1400s Gold leaf is used in Spain as a dental filling.

◄ **Henry the Navigator, the Portuguese prince who particularly encouraged exploration.**

1400s By now alchemists are no longer considered to be wise scholars, but instead they have the reputation of being con-artists and swindlers.

c. 1400 Abyssinians (Ethiopians) make contact with European rulers: a letter from King Henry IV of England (ruled 1399–1413) answering one from the Emperor of Abyssinia survives.

1415 Spain and Portugal launch the "Age of Discovery" when European explorers voyage along the coast of Africa and reach the East Indies. The thrust is initially led by Portuguese princes.

◄ **The old bridge, the Ponte Vecchio in Florence, built in 1345 to replace an older version.**

1418 Jaoa Gonvalves Zarco of Portugal, blown off course, sights the island of Madeira, which is promptly colonized by Portugal.

1401 Lorenzo Ghiberti (1378–1455) is commissioned to create the north and east doors of the Florence baptistry, an event often used by Italians to signify the end of the Middle Ages.

1410 John, Duke of Berry in France commissions a magnificent illustrated prayer book or book of hours known as *Les Très Riches Heures du Duc de Berry* (*The Very Rich Hours of the Duke of Berry*).

15th century The Renaissance is taking place in Italy.

A range of hennin headresses. ►

1400 The conical *hennin* headress is popular. ❀ Northern Italian cities develop differing methods of ruling and take control of their surrounding regions in most of northern Italy. Florence is a republic, Milan is a despotism, and Venice is ruled by a merchant council.

1400s Scholars first use the term "Middle Ages" to describe the years from the decline of the Western Roman Empire until their own period.

◄ **One of the beautiful pages from *Les Très Riches Heures du Duc de Berry*.**

1425 Great Feudal War in Russia – civil war for control of Moscow.

1429 Joan of Arc leads French forces to relieve English siege of Orléans. Joan is captured in 1430, charged as a witch by the English and on 30 May, 1431 she is burned to death in Rouen.

The death of Joan of Arc. ▼

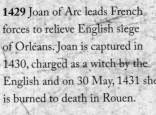

1438–41 Dutch–Hanseatic War. Dutch merchants break the Hanseatic League's trading monopoly.

1443 Skenderbeg leads Albanian resistance to Ottomans and pushes the Turks out of the country.

1443–90 Life of Hunyadi's son Matthias Corvinus, at different times king of Hungary, Croatia, Bohemia, and Duke of Austria, who fights against the Ottoman invasion.

1453 End of the Hundred Years' War. ✸ Ottoman Turks under Sultan Mehmet II conquer Constantinople, effectively bringing to an end the 1000-year-old Eastern Roman Empire.

1454 Italy comprises 5 major regions: the Papal States, Florence, Venice, Milan, and the kingdom of Naples.

1455–87 Wars of the Roses: civil war in England between Houses of York and Lancaster. The Princes in the Tower are murdered, hunchback Richard III takes the throne, but eventually Henry Tudor (I) becomes king. Many English historians use this to define the end of the Middle Ages.

English lords choose red or white roses to symbolize their support in the Wars of the Roses. ▶

1438–45 Council of Florence. Attempts to reunite Eastern and Roman churches fails.

1438–9 Printing press developed by Johannes Gutenberg in Germany.

1427 Thomas à Kempis writes *The Imitation of Christ*.

1427 Portuguese sailors sight the Azores, which become an important landfall for long-distance voyages.

▲ The late medieval astronomical clock of Prague Castle. By now European clockmakers are skilled and sophisticated.

1434 Portuguese sailors round the promontory of Cape Bojador in West Africa.

1452–98 Life of Girolamo Savonarola, reformer and critic of corruption amongst the papacy. He establishes a Christian democracy in Florence in 1494 but is brought down by the church and burnt at the stake.

1456–62 Rule of Vlad III, or the Impaler, in Wallachia, now part of Romania. He struggles against the Ottoman invasion of the Balkans.

Girolamo Savonarola. ▶

1444 By now African slaves have been brought to Europe by the Portuguese.

A medieval depiction of one of King Arthur's knights. ▶

c.1450 Birth of Spanish Jewish astronomer Abraham Zacuto.

c.1455 First printed book in Europe: Johannes Gutenberg's Bible.

c.1430–1512 Life of French Gothic sculptor Michel Colombe.

The inside of Brunelleschi's dome of Santa Maria del Fiore, the Florence cathedral. ▼

1436 Felippo Brunelleschi completes the dome of Florence cathedral.

1450s–70 English knight Sir Thomas Malory collects Arthurian legends into *Le Morte D'Arthur* (The Death of Arthur).

1452 Birth of Leonardo da Vinci.

1450s The Popes plan to rebuild St. Peter's Basilica in Rome, the heart of the Vatican.

15th century By now the Renaissance has begun in Italy. With intellectual and economic development, Europe begins to take center stage in world affairs.

1450 The population of Europe is about 50 million. It has not yet recovered from the devastation of the Black Death.

1461 Fall of Trebizond to the Ottomans. The Byzantine Empire ceases to exist. Louis XI of France enforces his control over the whole country after the chaos of the 100 Years War, and sets French kings on the path of absolute monarchy.

1474 Swiss Confederation and Habsburgs sign peace treaty.

1480 Mongols are unable to force the Russian state based in Moscow to pay tribute. Ivan III of Russia declares himself independent.

1487 Tudor rule in England sees new political and social institutions that show the Middle Ages are over.

1462 Spanish peasants revolt in First Rebellion of the Remencas and win some reforms.

1477 Battle of Nancy signals the end of the Duchy of Burgundy. Its lands become part of the Kingdom of France or, in the Burgundian Netherlands, are soon ruled by the Habsburgs.

1478 Moscow defeats Poland for control of the independent trading state Novgorod.

DRACULA

The historical personality on whom Victorian novelist Bram Stoker based his character "Dracula" was a southern Romanian or Wallachian warlord who fought against the Ottoman incursion of the Balkans, and also against the then-powerful and expanding Hungarian Empire.

Born in 1431, the son of prince (voivode) Vlad II Dracul of Wallachia, Dracula was also known as Vlad Tepes (the Impaler). His father was a member of the Holy Roman Empire's knightly Order of the Dragon, so was called in Romanian "Dracul." Thus, the younger Vlad was known as Dracula – son of the Dragon. Barbaric even for his time, Dracula was known for impaling thousands of his enemies.

1478 The Spanish Inquisition is formed to seek out converted Jews and Muslims who secretly continue with their old faiths. For many years it is led by Tomas de Torquemada (1420–98).

▲ **A procession of penitants convicted by the Inquisition.**

The knight and scholar Earl Rivers met the printer William Caxton when in exile in Europe. On their return to England, one of Caxton's first printed books was Rivers' translation of *Sayings of Sayings of the Philosophers*. Here they present a copy of the book to King Edward IV. ▶

1476 William Caxton sets up a printing press in London, England.

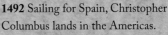

▲ **The warlord Vlad Tepes, possibly the historical figure behind the legend of Dracula.**

1469 Birth of Niccolo Machiavelli, who goes on to write *The Prince.*

1460 Portuguese settle on the Cape Verde islands off western Africa.

◀ **A page from Gutenberg's Bible, the first printed book in Europe.**

1487–8 Portuguese explorer Bartolomeu Dias rounds the southern cape of Africa.

1492 Sailing for Spain, Christopher Columbus lands in the Americas.

1494 Treaty of Tordesillas. Spain and Portugal agree to accept Pope Alexander VI's division of the New World between them in return for converting the heathens.

1497 Sailing for England, John Cabot crosses the Atlantic and lands in what is now Canada.

1498 The Portuguese explorer Vasco da Gama sails around the southern tip of Africa and reaches India.

1473 Sistine Chapel is built in the Vatican.

1475 Birth of Michelangelo.

◀ **Christopher Columbus arrives in the Caribbean.**

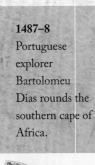

1475 Blood libel of Simon of Trent (Trento in Italy) leads to massacre of Jews there.

1484 Pope Innocent VII appoints Heinrich Kramer and Johann Sprenger as inquisitors in Germany. They write *Malleus Maleficarum* (*Hammer of the Witches*), the guide to identifying witches.

1492 Muslim rule in Spain comes to an end as Ferdinand of Aragon and Isabella of Castile conquer the last Moorish kingdom of Grenada. They demand that Jews convert or leave. Jews expelled from Sicily.

◀ **An astrolabe, one of the navigational instruments that enabled explorers to cross the oceans.**

1496 Portugal expels Jews.

CHARLEMAGNE'S EMPIRE

THE FORGING OF FRANCE AND GERMANY

France was one of the most important countries in the European Middle Ages, emerging at different times as one of the continent's leading states and influencing other nations.

This trend began soon after the retreat of Roman troops when people of one of the Germanic tribes, the Franks, moved into the area and became Romanized (or Gallicized). The developing Frankish kingdom adopted the trappings of Roman administration, and while much of the rest of Europe fell into disarray, this central kingdom became a beacon of relative stability and security.

THE MEROVINGIANS

We know nothing about the Frankish leader Merovech except for his name, which gave rise to the Merovingian dynasty, the first royal house of France and the first great "barbarian" kingdom in northern Europe. Merovech's grandson Clovis became leader of the tribe in 481 at the age of 15, and immediately began to consolidate his rule by killing rival members of his family. From his base at Tournai in what is now Belgium he united several other tribes into a Frankish kingdom covering the northern part of modern France and the southwestern part of modern Belgium. Clovis, whose name evolved into the popular royal French name Louis, then expanded further by pressing into southern Gaul (the Roman name for France), pushing the Visigoths there across the Pyrenees into what is now Spain.

Clovis converted to Roman Catholicism, married a Burgundian princess, and moved his capital to Paris. There he had the ancient law code of the Salian Franks written down in the hope of establishing it over his wide territory. In a gesture that acknowledged Clovis' influence, the eastern Roman emperor Anastasius gave him the status of consul, a senior official rank of ancient Rome.

Upon Clovis' death his kingdom was divided between his sons and eventually separated into two: Austrasia, which was approximately Clovis' original holding in Belgium and northeast France; and Neustria (meaning "new"). Burgundy was the other important power in the region.

The Merovingian dynasty ruled for 200 years before one of the royal advisors, or "mayors of the palace," Pepin II, took effective control of all three states as advisor. But he left civil war in his wake when he died in 714. It was 13 years before Pepin's illegitimate son, Charles, defeated all his enemies and took control of the Frankish lands. Nicknamed Martel ("the Hammer") because of his military abilities, the new dynasty took its name from the Latin, Carolus, for Charles.

THE CAROLINGIANS

Charles Martel encouraged the missionary work of St. Boniface amongst the tribes from Fresia and Saxony who were always encroaching upon the Franks, but the biggest threat came from the southwest, from the Arabs and Berbers who had conquered Spain and a strip of southern France along the Mediterranean. From there the Muslims were constantly raiding and testing the Franks. At the Battle of Tours or Poitiers in 732 Charles Martel halted the Muslim advance, pushing them back permanently to southern France. At that point he was still maintaining the illusion that he was just a mayor of the palace, and that his puppet king, the Merovingian Childeric III was the real ruler.

Charles' son Pepin III (the Short) continued this pretence until, with the

Top: Clovis I.
Bottom: Pepin the Short.

agreement of the Pope, he deposed the Merovingians and took the throne. In 754 he was annointed by Pope Stephen II, a moment that was acknowledged in the coronation of every French monarch from then until the French Revolution. In turn Pepin helped the Pope reclaim territory that had been taken from him by the Lombard kingdom in Italy, and form his lands into the Papal States. The process of dividing Italy into small states was well under way.

Pepin then went on to reclaim the Languedoc in southern France from the Muslims, exert control over Aquitaine, and expand into Germany before his death in 768.

CHARLES THE GREAT

Born in 742, Pepin's son Charles conquered the Lombard kingdom in France and northern Italy, expanded through Germany south into Pannonia (now Hungary) where he began to clash with the Byzantine empire, and north through Saxony to the Elbe. A pious Christian, his expansion was driven in part by his desire to baptize the pagan tribes of Germany and further east. Called "the Great" or Charlemagne, he created a huge Frankish state, the only empire to ever unite France and Germany, which contained parts or all of what we now call northeast Spain, France, Belgium, Germany, the Netherlands, Switzerland, Austria, and north Italy. Charlemagne's influence on Europe was enormous:

Charlemagne shown as a statue at St. Louis Cathedral, Rome.

Charles Martel at the Battle of Tours.

- His kingdom was an island of stability and security amongst chaos and uncertainty.
- The feudal system stemmed from his allocation of land: he promised to give territory under his rule to the fighters who supported him in battle.
- He directed a central administration of the empire through governors or counts (from the Latin for companion), and annual inspectors.
- He organized annual ceremonies for lords and officials to renew their oaths of fealty.
- He enforced law throughout the kingdom but respected national customs.
- He established monasteries with schools attached.
- He attracted learned men and encouraged a revival of scholarship and arts known as the Carolingian Renaissance.
- His good relations with the Pope and belief that rulers should be inspired by God cemented a Church-State relationship that lasted centuries.
- He opened diplomatic relations with many countries, including Anglo-Saxon kingdoms in Britain, Christians in Palestine, and the Arab caliph Haroun al-Raschid in Baghdad.
- He was the first new Western Roman Emperor.

Charles did, however, fail in his expedition to Spain, when an intended alliance with one of the Muslim governors collapsed and he had to retreat. His army was defeated en route by the Vascons or Basques at Roncesvalles in 778, an event immortalized in the later *Song of Roland*, commemorating the death there of Charlemagne's nephew Roland.

But his towering influence over Christian Europe was recognized in Rome on Christmas Day, 800 when Pope Leo III crowned him Emperor of the Romans. It was a symbolic moment that recognized Charlemagne's status as ruler over many different conquered people; it thanked him for his self-adopted role as protector of the Pope; it hearkened

CAROLVS MAGNVS

In 843 Charlemagne's three grandsons fought over their inheritance and then, at the Treaty of Verdun, agree to divide the kingdom between them. They created states that foreshadowed modern nations and laid the foundations for western Europe as we know it. The new kingdoms were:

- West Francia or Frankia (parts of modern France)
- Middle Francia
- East Francia (parts of modern Germany and Austria), which gradually took over the Middle Kingdom north of the Alps, leaving the rest in northern Italy.

The title of Roman Emperor was used by whichever ruler was best able to protect the popes – in general the ruler of the Middle Kingdom, and therefore, later, the king of East Francia. The Treaty of Verdun had to be written in two languages, because already West Francia was speaking the old French that would see their country's name Latinized into France, while the East Franks had a Germanic language.

For the next hundred years the kings of West Francia or France declined in power as aristocrats settled on their allotted territories and challenged royal authority. In East Francia the authority of the kings was also weakened by the rise of regional powers known as the stem duchies: Bavaria, Franconia, Lorraine, Saxony, and Swabia. But the futures of France and Germany were to differ enormously from then on.

Left: Charlemagne depicted in stained glass in Cologne Cathedral.
Below: The coronation of Charlemagne.

back to the stability and glory of the Roman empire, and from the Pope's point of view it had the happy side-effect of thoroughly annoying his rivals in the Byzantine Eastern Roman empire.

THE CAROLINGIAN RENAISSANCE

The Anglo-Saxon Benedictine monk Alcuin, a student of Bede, oversaw the copying of classic Latin documents, the establishment of a library and schools, and the invention of a new, more readable style of writing that many centuries later became italic. Illuminated gospels were a feature of the period, and by looking towards ancient Rome for inspiration, the seeds were sown for Romanesque architecture.

Cities of the Carolingian empire were small, and mainly served as administrative centers for the king or grew up around a monastery or trade market. In general, the artistic and literary movement was largely confined to the clergy, and, like the empire itself, did not survive long after Charlemagne's death in 814.

Charlemagne's Empire
  Treaty of Verdun, 843
  Great Fiefs

ABBREVIATIONS:
KDM......Kingdom
DM......Dukedom
M..........Margraviate
CO.........Countship

Clockwise from top left: Scribes copied texts for Charlemagne's library. Decor on the facade of Aachen Cathedral, Germany, where Charlemagne was buried and where German kings and queens were crowned for hundreds of years. Charlemagne's empire, showing the divisions into three kingdoms of the Treaty of Verdun.

FRANCE

In 987 a new dynasty, that of Hugh Capet, Duke of France and Count of Paris, succeeded the Carolingians in the West Francia kingdom that was to become France. The monarchy was weakened when Viking invaders raided almost at will up the great rivers, attacking Paris and seizing the region that became known as Normandy – the land of the Northmen. Rollo, the Viking leader, eventually agreed to give nominal allegiance to the French king, but for many years the rulers of France were able to do little more than hold on to the territories they held as personal, familial lands.

THE GREAT DISTRICTS OF FRANCE

- Aquitaine
- Brittany
- Champagne
- Burgundy
- Normandy

The Capetian royal family held lands around Paris and elsewhere. Including later branches of

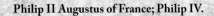

Philip II Augustus of France; Philip IV.

the houses of Valois and Bourbon, they would rule France for centuries. But in the mid-twelfth century it seemed for a time that they would be overwhelmed by the English.

Prince Henry of England, later Henry II, inherited Normandy through his mother, Mathilda of England, and the County of Anjou from his father, Geoffrey of Anjou. In 1152 he married Eleanor of Aquitaine, who had recently divorced King Louis VII of France. She had inherited Aquitaine, and after allying with Brittany, Henry now ruled half of France. His son John, however, lost much of his land to Philip II Augustus of France, and in 1214 after the Battle of Bouvines the English kings only controlled the Duchy of Guyenne (Aquitaine) in the south west. Philip II not only extended his territory, he also improved government, and it was during his reign that the monarch was referred to not as king of the Franks, but as king of France. The Albigensian Crusades against heretics in the Languedoc also led to an expansion of French rule and by 1300 modern France was taking shape, with only a few areas such as Brittany and Burgundy still independent.

ST. LOUIS

When France next took center stage in Europe it was led by a saint. King Louis IX, born in 1214, ascended to the throne in 1226, when his mother, Blanche of Castile, acted as his regent.

Louis' reign was called the "golden century," a time when France was Europe's leading country in terms of politics, economy, the military, and in the arts. Louis was devout, just, and generous. Regarded as a perfect Christian prince, he was respected by his peers and often chosen to judge quarrels. France was not only the biggest country in the continent, it was also the wealthiest, and Louis was able to patronize artists from the painters who illustrated the Morgan Bible to the architects who built his personal chapel in Paris, the Sainte-

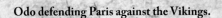

Odo defending Paris against the Vikings.

Louis IX on Crusade.

Chapelle, home of one of Christendom's most important relics, the Crown of Thorns. Gothic art developed greatly during his reign, and Parisian arts became highly sought after in other countries. French influences were also spread by the many dynastic marriages Louis arranged between his relatives and other European ruling families.

Louis died on crusade in 1270, leaving a prosperous country with improved administration and a tradition of glorious art. He was canonized in 1297.

PHILIP THE FAIR

Known as "le Bel" or the Fair because of his blond hair, St. Louis' grandson, Philip IV was another king who was concerned with expanding the territory and role of the monarch. Through dynastic marriages, purchases, or political maneuvring, Philip consolidated several territories within France including Toulouse, Lyon, and southern Flanders, as well as many small counties. Under him government bureaucracy grew, and, particularly in order to win support for the regular taxes he needed for his wars of expansion, he called large national assemblies, a foreshadowing of the future Estates-General or parliament of France.

Philip the Fair influenced Europe in two main ways: in 1307 he had French Templars arrested for heresy (possibly in order to seize their wealth), and convinced the pope to ban the order of knights in 1312. Templars were tortured until they confessed to heretical practices, and although many of them recanted their confessions, the grand master of the order was burnt at the stake. Philip did not, however, gain many riches. Perhaps forewarned, several Templars escaped with the bulk of their treasure, which vanished into history.

France under siege: foreign influences in 1430.

the popes were all, themselves, French. Only in 1377 did Pope Gregory XI move back to Rome.

By 1328 France could raise the largest army in Europe, had the biggest tax base, and was the most powerful kingdom in the continent. Only Brittany, Burgundy, Aquitaine, and Flanders were not directly controlled by the French monarch.

THE HUNDRED YEARS' WAR

Fought almost entirely in France, the Hundred Years' War from 1337 to 1453 saw the devastation of several parts of northern France. War was bad enough, but even during times of peace the countryside was subject to the depravations of mercenary troops, a new development that signaled the end of traditional feudal armies.

The Hundred Years' War introduced several changes that contributed to the end of the Middle Ages and the dawn of the modern era. In warfare, artillery was used on such a scale that it completely changed the nature of sieges. Castles, which had been the symbol of local power for centuries, were suddenly vulnerable, and town walls offered no defenses against cannon. Open warfare also changed, since the introduction of crossbows and the fire-power of the longbow cut down the charges of mounted knights.

The war ended with France gaining all of England's continental possessions except Calais, and with the French monarchy in a more dominant position over the dukes, counts, and princes of the land.

GERMANY AND THE HOLY ROMAN EMPIRE

The Middle Ages saw many of today's European nation-states coalesce and emerge. Germany took a different route, with powerful independent territories only loosely united under a Holy Roman Emperor.

After the Treaty of Verdun in 843 East Francia, covering most of modern Germany and Austria, went its separate way from the West Frankish Kingdom that was to become France. Soon the monarchs found that their status and influence was eroded by powerful regions known as the stem duchies: Bavaria, Franconia, Lorraine, Saxony, and Swabia. Over time many German lords were so powerful they took on the title of princes, but although the monarchy weakened, territorially the kingdom eventually took over most of the Middle Frankish Kingdom north of the Alps.

THE SAXON DYNASTY

In East Francia the last king of Charlemagne's line died in 911, and the German dukes elected their new king, Conrad, Duke of Franconia, establishing a lasting tradition. Although Henry I of Saxony (ruled 919–36) was able to appoint his son Otto as the next king, the principle of electing a king distinguished German politics for centuries.

Otto I became known as the Great as he strengthened the monarchy, encouraged German expansion into parts of Slavic Bohemia and Poland to the east, and stopped the advance of the Magyars at the battle of Lechfeld in 955.

THE HOLY ROMAN EMPIRE

In 962 the Pope crowned Otto king of the Romans, beginning the expectation that the elected king of the Germans would be also be crowned the Holy Roman Emperor, as the title became.

The title gave German kings huge prestige within Christendom. It also affected

Above: Otto the Great and his Seal.
Right: The crown of the Holy Roman Empire.

development in Germany: since the kings were often away attending to their Italian holdings, the German nobles became ever more powerful at the expense of the monarchy.

THE INVESTITURE CONTROVERSY

Pope and emperor began as two strands that worked together to defend Christendom. However their close relationship broke down in 1075 over who had the right to appoint or invest members of the German church. Known as the Investiture Controversy or Contest, it pitted the reforming pope, Gregory VII, against Henry IV (reigned 1056–1106), and saw war devastate Germany from 1070 until 1122.

Pope Gregory questioned the idea of the divine right of kings, demanded that Henry give up all rights to investiture in the German church, and threatened to excommunicate any church officials who supported the king. Always keen to limit the power of the emperors, many German nobles took the side of the pope.

In 1077 Henry visited the pope to give penance and receive absolution. Their reunion was short-lived however, as he then continued to invest officials, and sought for the election of an antipope.

THE CONCORDAT OF WORMS

Peace was only reached in 1122 with the Concordat of Worms, accepting that the pope had the authority to appoint church officials, but the German king had the right of veto. By then the struggle had further weakened the power of the monarchy at the expense of local lords, who increased their followings by taking oaths of homage from previously free men fleeing the chaos of civil war.

WELFS AND HOHENSTAUFENS

In 1125 the dukes elected Lothair II, of the Saxon family Welf (Guelf). This began spread when the Welfs sided with the popes and Italian city-states against the Hohenstaufen dynasty.

Hohenstaufen kings such as Frederick Barbarossa and Frederick II were strong, dynamic figures, but still the regional lords wielded power within the empire, although a particular aspect of German nobility was the division of their lands into ever smaller parcels.

Then, from 1273 with the election of Rudolf of Habsburg a new pattern emerged. From then on the emperor came from one of three houses: Luxemburg (from Bohemia), Wittelsbach (from Bavaria), or Habsburg (from Austria), who kept the crown from the mid-fifteenth century onwards.

THE GOLDEN BULL

Named after the golden seal that was fixed to it, this document of 1356 was a mainstay of German politics and kingship for 400 years. It specified the seven electors of the "king to be promoted emperor": three senior churchmen of Mainz, Trier, and Cologne; four dukes of Bohemia, Palsgrave, Saxony, and Brandenburg. For the first time in Germany, the Bull allowed for a majority vote, and it also specified that the four electing states should not be divided.

COLONIZATION

In the twelfth and thirteenth centuries Germany expanded eastwards into Slavic lands. The Teutonic Order of warrior-monks also began crusades or wars of conquest in the east, suffering a defeat by Poland at the Battle of Tannenberg in 1410, but continuing to press on until they were disbanded in the sixteenth century.

CULTURE

The Investiture Contest had an additional effect of delaying Germany's cultural and intellectual development compared with France and Italy. German culture did, however, spring to glorious life during the reign of Frederick I Barbarossa (r. 1152-90), with the flowering of lyrical love poetry, epic narratives, and courtly love expressed by the Minnesingers.

From the thirteenth century Germany also saw the rise of the Hanseatic League, a union of trading cities that grew to dominate maritime trade in the Baltic and throughout north Europe.

RELIGIOUS CONFLICT

Late Medieval Germany saw the rise

Left: Gold plate from the shrine of St. Severinus in Cologne, around 1090.
Center: A well-dressed German noble family in 1180.
Right: Emperor Henry IV and his sons.

of religious dissension, typified by the Czech reformer Jan Hus or John Huss (c.1372–1415) in Bohemia. A follower of Englishman John Wycliffe who condemned corruption within the Church and translated the Bible into the vernacular so that more people could read it, Hus was an important precursor of the sixteenth-century Reformation that changed the face of Christianity. He was burnt at the stake, but his followers went on to influence the cause of Protestant Reformation in Europe.

Germany, 1377
- Habsburg
- Luxemburg
- Wittelsbach
- Ecclesiatical

Above: Germany in the 14th century.
Left: Emperor Frederick Barbarossa.
Right: Emperor Frederick II.

VIKING EXPANSION

Known as the Age of the Vikings, the years from 793 to 1066 saw seafaring pirates from Scandinavia raid coastal and river settlements in Scotland, Ireland, England, and France.

The marauders also struck at will down the Danube into the heart of Europe, along the coastline to Portugal, and even crossed the Atlantic Ocean.

The Scandinavians traded with and explored or colonized Kiev in the Ukraine, Byzantium, Iceland, Greenland, and North America. Although known as brutal murderers and plunderers, Viking life was broader than that. They were excellent administrators of the towns and colonies they founded, had a vibrant artistic culture, and a complex system of laws.

Although there were earlier raids, the Viking Age itself dates from their 793 attack on the monastery on Lindisfarne off northeast England, and ends with Harold Hardrada's failed attempt to conquer England in 1066. During those centuries much of Europe was terrorized by the iconic longships and armed warriors.

In the early Middle Ages Scandinavia was not divided into its modern states of Norway, Sweden, and Denmark. Those national kingdoms arose at the end of the Viking period, when the pope legitimized Christian rulers. Before then local chieftains controlled fluid areas, and although some raids were carried out by Vikings from a particular area of what is now Denmark or Norway, the major expeditions of hundreds of ships involved adventurers from all over Scandinavia.

The term Viking comes from the Old Norse "vikingr" and may originally have meant a seaman from the Vik region of the fjord of Oslo in Norway. However by 1000 it was used for any Scandinavian raider. Alternatively, it has been suggested that the word derives from one who hides in a "vik" or bay, that is, a pirate.

CAUSES OF THE RAIDS

Scandinavian communities were harsh and self-sufficient, but in the late eighth century Vikings realized that they could gain wealth and luxuries by raiding elsewhere. Few towns were rich,

Above: A runestone, marked with the Scandinavians' angular letters.
Below: Longships at sea. The warriors hung their shields on the sides of the ships.

but monasteries were often the centers for local trade, and as well as housing the Church's wealth, locals lords stored their treasure there. Killing and burning as they went, Vikings began to swoop down upon these treasure-houses, taking gold, silver, and slaves.

Instead of selling their plunder elsewhere, Vikings often held it to ransom, selling church treasures back to the monasteries. But many institutions were destroyed, and monks eventually abandoned vulnerable sites such as Lindisfarne and Iona.

Those Northmen who settled in other countries were probably forced out of Scandinavia by lack of land, or because a local chieftain was expanding his territory. Rather than fighting back, it was easier to set sail and conquer lands in another country.

THE SEAFARERS

In the late eighth century there were no navies left in European waters, and longships had the seas to themselves. The best shipbuilders of the time, the Vikings crafted strong, fast boats. A sturdy keel gave support to the mast but allowed the ships to be both sailed or rowed, and with a flat bottom, the longships could sail in shallow coastal waters and reach far up major rivers. Navigation relied mainly upon tracking the movement of the sun.

SETTLEMENTS IN NORTHERN EUROPE

In the ninth century Vikings colonized the Scottish islands of the Orkneys and Shetlands as well as parts of northern Scotland and Ireland, particularly Dublin. Then, amassing an army, they invaded England. York fell in 866, and by 878 nearly all of England was under their control. Only King Alfred of Wessex remained at large, and his dynasty began the process of reclaiming England. The last Viking king of York, Eric Bloodaxe, was finally expelled in 954.

In 879 Vikings began to colonize Iceland, which became the springboard for the settlement of Greenland in 980. Then, in 1000 they reached what is today Newfoundland in Canada, founding a short-lived settlement at L'Anse aux Meadows.

DANEGELD

In the late tenth century a new phase of Viking terror began. Led by the Danes under Harald Bluetooth, the Vikings began a process of "extortion," demanding money to stop them attacking. For decades English kings made these payments, known as Danegeld, but their submission did not stave off an attack, for in 1013 Harald's son, Swein Forkbeard, invaded. His son Canute (Cnut) completed the conquest, and in 1027

A reconstruction of a long, thatched Viking house.

he announced himself as "king of the whole of England and Denmark and Norway and of parts of Sweden."

Partly to legitimize his reign, Canute married Emma, the widow of the last Saxon English king, Aethelred (the Unready). She was a daughter of the duke of Normandy, the descendant of another Viking line, and her son, the future king Edward the Confessor, was the connection between the English throne and the Normans that led to the Norman Conquest of 1066.

NORMANDY

In 885 a Viking fleet penetrated the Seine river as far as Paris, besieging the city. They were "paid off," but did not abandon France altogether, and eventually the chieftain Hrolf or Rollo settled in Normandy, agreeing a nominal allegiance to the French crown. Taking the Christian name Robert, his descendants became the dukes of Normandy.

EASTERN EUROPE

Across the Baltic Sea Vikings reached Poland, Latvia, Lithuania, and Russia. Fleets sailing down rivers such as the Volga engaged in trade as well as piracy, and also formed colonies from the 750s onwards. In what is now Ukraine they founded the Rus state around Kiev, extracting tribute from Slavic and Finnic tribes from 859, and giving their name to the future nation of Russia.

Above: The distinctive runic writing that developed in Scandinavia.
Left: The dragon was a popular subject for Viking art.

SICILY

Having raided and settled southern Italy for decades, an invasion force of Vikings crossed into Sicily in 1061, taking the city of Messina from its Arab garrison, then slowly taking control of the rest of the island. The Norman period was a golden age for Sicily, when Catholic and Orthodox Christians, Jews, and Muslims lived together peacefully, and the Kingdom of Sicily, which included large parts of southern Italy, became wealthy. The golden age lasted until 1250, after which the island was ruled by the Holy Roman Empire from Naples or further afield, and the Viking heritage in the country became entangled in Italy's development into small city-states.

been. Strong castles were built, in which the local population could seek refuge during a raid, and the development of mounted knights meant that there was now a viable challenge to the Viking warriors. At the same time, Vikings had to turn their attention to internal affairs, as Scandinavia became weakened by domestic unrest. The Age of the Vikings was over.

ΤΗΕ IMPACT OF THE VIKINGS

Destroyed or abandoned monasteries, enslaved communities, powerful kingdoms such as at York, all were features of the Viking Age. The constant raids had another major impact on some parts of Europe, particularly northern France, where the independent free peasant practically disappeared. Driven off their land by the regular Viking threat, these freemen often sought service with a powerful leader who might offer some protection against the Northmen. As a result, the land became polarized between the lords and serfs, with little in between.

Some of the routes followed by Viking marauders and traders.

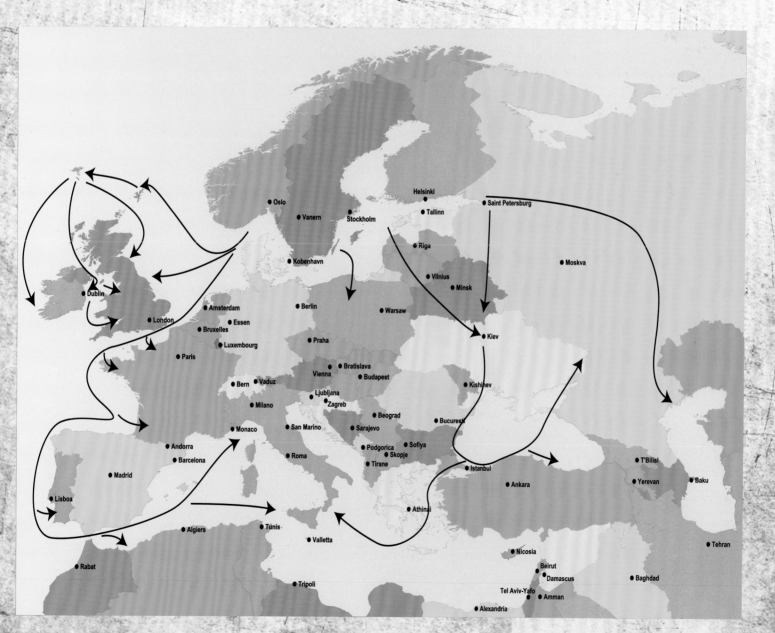

Normandy in northern France is named for the Northmen or Norse, the Vikings from Norway and other parts of modern Scandinavia who settled there in 911. Led by Rollo, who took the Christianized Latin name of Robert, the Normans eventually swore fealty to Charles III of France, and Rollo became the count or duke of Normandy.

Vikings also invaded Scotland, eastern England, Russia and southern Italy, forming new kingdoms and gaining a continent-wide reputation for ruthless military might.

The monarchy of eleventh-century northern Europe was a complicated web of marriages, alliances, and feuds. In England the Anglo-Saxon king St. Edward the Confessor succeeded the Danish king Harthacanut in 1047. With a Norman mother, Edward spent many years of his youth in exile in Normandy, and appeared to admire the society there. According to Norman sources, he swore an oath that the Norman duke would be his heir should he later achieve his aim of becoming king of England.

This was the basis of the Norman claim to the throne of England, a claim that was compounded by the visit of another Anglo-Saxon, the earl of Wessex Harold Godwinson, whose family were sworn enemies of Edward's family. According to Norman chroniclers, Harold also took an oath of support to the then duke of Normandy, William II, who would go on to be the Conqueror William I of England. The Saxons argued that

Harold swearing an oath on a Holy Relic to support William.

if Harold had indeed sworn allegiance, he did so only under duress, so the oath was not valid.

THE BATTLE OF HASTINGS

Edward the Confessor died in early 1066, and to William's fury, Harold Godwinson was crowned the next king of England. Ambitious and ruthless, William prepared an invasion force. His fleet of 777 ships – dragon-prowed like the Viking ships of old – carried about 7,000 mounted knights and foot soldiers to land near Pevensey on the south coast of England on September 28, 1066.

Left: William the Conqueror in action as depicted on the Bayeux Tapestry.
Above: The death of Harold as shown on the Bayeux Tapestry.

Three days earlier, King Harold had defeated another invading army, that of Harald Hardrada from Norway. The English had marched from London north to Stamford Bridge in Yorkshire to fight this force, and barely caught their breath before they had to rush back to the southern coast to meet the Normans.

Harold's army took just four days to cross 200 miles before encountering the invasion force near Hastings on October 14. The English took up a defensive position on the top of a hill, and for several hours fought off the attacking Normans, many of whom were on horseback while the English fought on foot. The turning point was a mistake: a cry went up that William had fallen, and the English pushed down from their high point. But William was still alive and kicking, and rallied his troops to slaughter the suddenly exposed English. With one final flurry of Norman arrows, Harold was struck in the face, and the English crumpled and scattered.

William marched on to London, and on Christmas Day 1066 he was crowned king in the grand, new Westminster Abbey.

THE BAYEUX TAPESTRY

A pictorial account of the invasion of England and the events that led up to it, this is the only surviving piece of its type from the eleventh century. A massive 230 feet long and 20 inches high, it took four years to complete, from 1088 to 1092. Probably designed by an artist, the scenes were then embroidered onto heavy linen, using threads of eight different colors. It may have been commissioned by William's half-brother, Odo, bishop of Bayeux, and is displayed in that town today.

WILLIAM THE CONQUEROR

Born probably in 1028 in Falaise, Normandy, William was the illegitimate son of Robert, duke of Normandy (known as "the Devil") and Herleve, the daughter of a tanner. Robert had

no other sons so, although William's parents never married, William was named heir to the duchy, and became duke when he was only seven or eight.

Resented by the other Norman lords, it was not long before William was fleeing for his life and the duchy fell into civil war. Although young, William showed those qualities he was to become famous for: military leadership, inner strength, determination, fierce loyalty to his friends, and utter ruthlessness towards his enemies.

By the time he was 20 he had rallied enough supporters to his side that, with the help of the French king Henry I, he defeated his rivals at the battle of Val-ès-Dunes near Caen in 1047. A warrior king, he was well known for his fighting skills. They were needed again soon, as the Count of Anjou began to threaten Normandy and a faction started to call William their "tanner." His response was to hack off the arms and legs of everyone who had mocked him, a move that made his enemies approach him much more warily from then on.

William faced other invasions of his duchy, including one assisted by his former friend Henry. But William fought off all attacks, strengthened his grip on his lands, and made new alliances, not least by marrying Matilda, daughter of the powerful count Baldwin of Flanders. Finally, in 1057, the constant incursions into Normandy by other magnates came to an end and the duchy enjoyed a period of peace.

William believed in strong government and imposed a rule of law firmly, even harshly. He was also deeply devout and founded many new monasteries.

Left: The Saxon church of St. Lawrence, Bradford-on-Avon, Wiltshire. Few Saxon churches remain because the Normans tended to knock them down and build on top.
Right: The Tower of London, symbol of Norman dominance.

NORMAN BRITAIN

CASTLES AND CONTROL

Immediately after the Norman conquest the invaders began to enforce their grip on the country. In true feudal fashion, William gave the lands of the dead Saxon lords to his followers – both Norman and French – and before long the Normans owned nearly all the great estates. They built castles as their homes in order to dominate the surrounding countryside; they fortified towns; and, where they felt it necessary, they devastated the land. After an uprising in 1069 the Norman conquerors killed more than 100,000 men, women, and children in the north of England, destroying villages and churning up farmland so that the region took ten years to recover. Known as the Harrying of the North, this brutal suppression showed that the Normans were there to stay.

William must have felt fairly confident of his invasion, for he had packed three portable wooden castles on his ships. These and other early wooden structures were soon replaced by stone, however, changing the face of the land. By the 1070s

work was underway on the stone White Tower, the first phase of the Tower of London to be the Conqueror's stronghold in that city. And in the countryside, a church was built beside the new lord's domain and new villages began to cluster there. Here the formerly free Saxons found that they were now practically enslaved as serfs, forced to pay fees and do work for their new landowners.

THE DOMESDAY BOOK

The Normans recorded every inch of their new kingdom in an important historical document, the Domesday Book. Begun in 1086, this is a complete survey of land ownership, carried out mainly so that William could assess taxes

Above: The church at Wootton Wawen, Warwickshire. The village is mentioned in the Domesday Book as containing "23 villagers with a priest and 22 smallholders."
Below: The village of Much Wenlock in Shropshire was recorded in the Domesday Book as Wenloch.

but as a result giving an extraordinary snapshot of medieval life, from the size of great estates down to how many pigs a peasant owned.

NORMAN ENGLAND

England's position in Europe changed completely with the Norman conquest. Its kings now had a unusual status in France. First of all they were still dukes of Normandy and had other lands in France, therefore nominally owed allegiance to the French monarchs. But they were not only mere vassals, for they were also brother kings. From the French crown's point of view the question of relative status often muddled even more because the tangled marriage and inheritance ties of the powerful Norman and French families meant that at times the English kings would lay claim to the French throne.

For some kings, such as Richard I (the Lionheart), England was considered to be just a backwater, and their main interest was in their continental holdings. New alliances and new conflicts were to follow.

Within England the Normans introduced the feudal system, with a strict hierarchy in society, new religious monasteries, as well as a new language – Norman-French – which began to dominate upper-class life. It took centuries before the Normans became "English," and the Latin-French and Anglo-Saxon-Germanic languages of the land merged together to form the middle English tongue. Norman kings attempted further expansion into Wales, Scotland, and Ireland, giving rise to centuries of conflict within Britain itself.

THE NORMAN DYNASTIES

William I, the Conqueror	reigned 1066–87
William II (Rufus)	1087–1100
Henry I	1100–35
Stephen	1135–54
Matilda	1141
Plantagenets	
Henry II	1154–89
Richard I the Lionheart	1189–99
John I	1199–1216
Henry III	1216–72
Edward I	1272–1307
Edward II	1307–27
Edward III	1327–77
Richard II	1377–99
The House of Lancaster	
Henry IV	1399–1413
Henry V	1413–22
Henry VI	1422–61, 1470–71
The House of York	
Edward IV	1461–70, 1471–83
Edward V	1483
Richard III	1483–85
The Tudors (1485–1603)	
Henry VII	1485–1509

MAGNA CARTA

In 1215 King John signed one of the first charters of liberties and rights, Magna Carta or "Great Charter." An unpopular king, John had raised taxes to pay for his wars in France, and had argued with the pope. The barons were on the point of rebellion when a compromise was reached and John signed the charter accepting that both lords and church had privileges that he would respect. He effectively agreed that even the king is subject to the law. The charter said: "to no one … will we deny or delay justice."

SCOTLAND

To most Scots England was the land of the Saxons, the Sassenachs. The accidental death of Scottish king Alexander III in 1289 set the stage for the Sassenachs (even though they were now Normans) to attempt to assimilate Scotland.

After civil war broke out over rival claims in Scotland, King Edward I of

Below left: The statue of Richard I outside the Houses of Parliament, London.
Below right: Effigy of King John.

England was asked to mediate. He manipulated events so that the eventual new king had to acknowledge Edward as overlord, and from then on England interfered with the Scottish throne. There were victories and political maneuvering on both sides until Robert the Bruce inflicted a decisive defeat on Edward II at Bannockburn in 1314, and in 1328 England finally recognized him as the independent king of Scotland.

WALES

Norman lords who were eager for new lands ventured into south Wales, carving out territory and defending it with a string of castles known as the Welsh Marches. Edward I also turned his attention to Wales, partly subduing the land, building more castles such as Caernarvon and Harlech, and making his son the new Prince of Wales, a title held by the eldest royal son ever since. There were rebellions, especially that led by Owen Glendower in 1400–9, but effectively Wales was now governed by England.

IRELAND

Once again the lands on the fringe of the conquered country were seen as potential territories by greedy Norman magnates, who invaded the island and created new fiefs for themselves. Nominally under the English king, they were left alone unless they challenged royal authority, but it was the beginning of English intervention in Irish affairs.

ENGLISH NATIONALISM

England's relations with France and other continental countries fluctuated. Henry II controlled huge territories in France, but soon after 1200 his son King John lost most of the family's French holdings, and, thrown back upon the British Isles, the

Top: Edward I.
Left: Robert the Bruce.
Below: Harlech Castle.

Norman overlords became more conscious of their separate identity as English. But Henry III married a sister of Louis IX of France, so was friendly with the leading European nation at the time.

Internal rebellions, demands for some form of parliamentary representation, and the impact of the Black Death all changed English society. Finally two major conflicts drained the country: the Hundred Years' War between England and France (1337–1453), which despite several English victories left the English kings only owning the city of Calais in France; and the Wars of the Roses (1455–85), when the rival houses of York and Lancaster fought for the throne.

Many historians say that the Wars of the Roses mark the end of the Middle Ages in Britain. The new Tudor dynasty would see world-shattering changes. But as peace fell in 1485 England was still medieval: of a population of just a few million, more than 95 percent of British people lived in the countryside.

Above left: Salisbury Cathedral, built from 1220 to 1258, is a prime example of English Gothic architecture and has Britain's tallest spire.
Above right: Stained glass windows in Salisbury Cathedral.
Left: King Edward IV with Richard, Duke of Gloucester.

THE FEUDAL SYSTEM

A way of allocating land according to service given, feudalism organized the lives of everyone from the king down to peasants or serfs.

Feudalism was the main social system in Europe during the ninth to the fifteenth centuries, replacing the earlier Roman state social structure with personal relationships between powerful people and the less powerful. Originating in Carolingian France when Charlemagne promised his followers that they would all be given parts of lands that would be conquered in the future, it became dominant in Europe by the time that the western part of the continent was fully Christianized.

The feudal system arranged society in a strict hierarchy, with royalty at the top giving lands to nobles or lords in exchange for their loyalty and service. The great lords held titles such as duke or count or baron and owned vast estates, sometimes scattered all over the country, in fact the word "feudal" derives from a Latin term for a particular land holding. In a pyramid system, the greater lords in turn took oaths of allegiance from lesser lords, their vassels, a lower level of nobility who held lesser titles, perhaps just lord or knight.

The main service expected of the lords was military, and at times of need they were required to supply their king with an agreed number of knights from within their own family or from among their own vassels, as well as a large force of ordinary men-at-arms. There were no standing armies for most of the Middle Ages, although the lords would have a few armed guardsmen. At times these would be augmented by ordinary free men who also owed the lord service.

THREE ORDERS

Society was effectively divided into three: those who fought (nobles and knights), those who prayed (churchmen), and those who labored.

VASSELS

In turn, the landowning nobles gave to their vassels smaller pieces of land to hold "in fee." The basic unit was known as a fee or fief, and would be big enough for a manor house or small castle, fields, woods, and whatever was needed for it to be self-sufficient, including serfs to do the work. Fiefs could be inherited upon payment of a new fee or tax to the lord or king. When King John of England sought to raise money by upping this fee he sparked a protest amongst the barons that led to the Magna Carta, a bill of rights for the lords.

If the family died out the overlord reclaimed the estate and allotted it to a new vassal to hold. Feudalism was such a strongly patriarchal and patrilineal system that if there was no male heir then the overlord would decide whether to allow a daughter to inherit, or whether to simply throw the survivors of the family off the land.

Through inheritance and marriage some families accumulated huge territories, taking as their family names the name of their estates. But for many periods it was the pope who was the largest feudal landlord of all, taking oaths of homage from thousands of subordinate landholders.

Above: A peasant.
Below: Workers busy on an estate while the lord looks on.

KINGSHIP

Medieval Europe thought that kingship mirrored the rightful relationships in Heaven, where God ruled, and that it was thus the most proper form of society. So kings ruled by a divine right, and just as vassals swore homage to their king or overlord, when a king was crowned he swore an oath to God.

Feudalism was all about who held land, and although kings at first ruled people, by the eleventh century it was firmly established that a king also ruled a particular territory, so national borders became more important to royalty than which families lived where.

Apart from military duties, a king might reward his vassals for other services such as good counsel or religious services, and over time, the personal royal courts that contained his advisers and chaplain priests evolved into national bureaucratic systems. The king ruled by might and the right of God, but he still often needed advice, and gatherings of counsellors became formalized into assemblies representing different orders of society, with – then just as now – taxation one of the most hotly debated topics. These councils varied from country to country, but were the embryonic forms of the British Parliament and the French Estates-General, among other later forms of national government.

FREEMEN

Commoners was a catch-all phrase for a number of different lower classes who were not serfs. There were a number of free peasants who were not bound to a particular fief, but in practice

Above left: Hunting and falconry were pleasurable pastimes for the nobles.
Above right: Feudalism centered around the countryside and rural pursuits.
Below left: Paying allegiance.
Below right: Kings and nobles had an official court jester to keep them entertained.

The arrival of Isabeau of Bavaria in Paris in 1385 as shown in Froissart's chronicle. Traveling in order to marry Charles VI of France, Isabeau and her entourage display all the wealth of nobles. Most of the women and men wear bright, fashionable clothes, but the man greeting Isabeau is wearing an old-fashioned robe for the formal occasion.

they did not move about much. Artisans and craftspeople such as millers, blacksmiths, and tailors were freemen or franklins, as were dedicated men-at-arms and general retainers. The term yeoman was often used for these.

SERFS

At the bottom of the social pyramid, the landless peasants, also known as serfs or villeins, were in many cases little better than slaves. Since serfs came with the land, they were tied to it, and did not perform military service, so were looked down upon by all. In return for their tiny plots of land that they lived on but did not actually own, they had to work a given number of days on the lord's estate, and were unable to leave the manor without permission. In the most restrictive cases, they could not marry outside the estate without permission, had to pay an annual "rent," and, on their parents' death, had to pay a fee in order to be able to carry on living on the land.

At times as much as 90 percent of the population worked as peasants. For them life was hard and short: few would live longer than 30 years of age. During those 30 years their work on the land supported the whole structure of the feudal system and made it possible for armored knights, the prized spearhead of medieval society, to lead a battle charge.

IN BRITAIN

Feudalism was introduced into Britain with the Norman Conquest in 1066, and was fiercely enforced by a rapid program of building castles and defensive walls around towns that soon managed to subdue local populations. Fortifications also offered protection, since in times of danger the population for miles around could flock to safety within the walls. As in other parts of Europe, these developments sometimes gave extra power and influence to the local lord at the expense of the centralized authority, the crown.

LAWS AND TAXES

At many times feudal lords had control of most local administrative and judicial systems. They could set most of their own laws and taxes, subject to very few restrictions from the monarchy. When a king tried to enforce central control, civil war might follow. Conversely, a very strong king like William the Conqueror could make it clear from the beginning exactly how much leeway he would allow his lords.

THE FEUDAL ECONOMY

Essentially based around ownership of land, the feudal period also saw a major change in the land-use of western Europe, from being centered around forests to being centered around farmed fields. At the beginning of the period the countryside was under-populated, and mainly consisted of small villages within woodlands, surrounded by unpopulated wastelands. But the population slowly began to grow, and this pressure for land, along with agricultural developments such as crop rotation, saw wastelands claimed by lords, and woods inexorably cut back to make room for more tilled land.

The lord of the manor owned everything. Peasants were required to use his mill (paying a fee), go to the local parish church (paying a tithe or tax to the priest), and sell their products only at the markets that he licensed (putting another fee in his pocket). But it was expensive to be a knight. Armor and warhorses, and the leisure time to train to use them, needed the material production of a whole estate.

DECLINE

The huge shock to society of the Black Death in 1348–50 was a major contributory factor to the decline of feudalism. So few workers survived that land-use began to change. Already, by then a money-based economy had arisen and begun to change the needs of landowners: instead of someone to work agricultural land they were more willing to let a serf buy his freedom, and use the land for other purposes.

With the growth of merchants and urban classes who did not own land but still had wealth, feudalism declined even further and gradually disappeared in western Europe by the end of the Middle Ages. In eastern Europe, however, it continued until the nineteenth century, and was only abolished in Russia in 1861.

Top: Working in the fields in the month of June. Behind the workers is the lord's great castle. From *Les Tres Riches Heures*.
Above left: The simple clothes and tools of peasants.
Above right: Everyday life for peasants immortalized in stained glass.

CASTLES

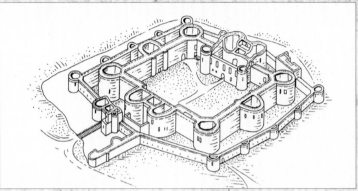

In the Middle Ages private residences of nobles were fortified for defense. They were called castles after the Latin "castellum," meaning military camp, and during the period as many as 100,000 castles were built in Europe. But castles were more than just a means of defense: they were a status symbol and a way of controlling hostile territories, and they were also used as administrative centers. Towns emerged within their shadows, encouraging trade and industry.

The first castles were built in France in the ninth century. This was a time of great turbulence when most of northern Europe was under constant attack from the Vikings, and local lords needed to find an effective means of defense. These castles were simple structures made of wood. A tower or keep was built on top of a raised earthwork called a "motte." Beneath the motte was the "bailey," an enclosed courtyard protected by a wooden palisade. In front of this a ditch was dug out, creating several layers of defense.

Motte and bailey castles were cheap to build and could be erected within a relatively short period of time. In times of peace the lord lived in the keep along with his family, while his servants and sergeants at arms were accommodated in the bailey. The design was so successful that within a hundred years motte and bailey castles were being built all over northern Europe. In Flanders, they were called vliedburg, or refuge castles.

THE NORMANS

The first castles in England were built by William I after the Norman Conquest. The largest of these still survives – the White Tower, the keep of the Tower of London. Built of stone, the White

Top: The first castles were motte and bailey, a wooden structure on a raised earth mound with an enclosed courtyard, surrounded by a water ditch.
Above: First developed in Crusader fortifications, concentric castles appeared. These had two separate defensive walls, an inner and an outer "curtain." The central stronghold began to disappear.
Below: In the late 13th century a new model of castle was developed, the enclosed castle, as at Bodiam in England. One large, wide, strong wall surrounding the structure, with a massive gatehouse and towers, all attached to the outer wall. The inner walls formed an enclosed courtyard, and instead of an inner keep the gatehouse-tower was used.

Above left: Defensive features of castles included narrow windows slits which protected defenders but allowed them to loose arrows at attacking forces.
Above right: This diagram shows the social divisions within a castle. The servants' hall with trestle tables was where many of them also slept. On the upper floor the lord's great hall and private apartments are more luxurious.
Below left: Moats, here at the mostly ruined Scotney Castle in England, gave an added circle of protection.
Below right: The restored Chateau de Roquetaillade, a square plan with crenelated towers and a large central keep.

Tower was completed in 1100 after 22 years of construction. It is 88 and a half feet high (27m) and was in its day the tallest structure in London. The White Tower was designed not only as a symbol of power but also as a means to intimidate the Anglo-Saxon population whom William had conquered in 1066.

In addition, the White Tower served as a jail. Its first prisoner was Ranulf Flambard, Bishop of Durham, jailed in 1101 on the charge of financial embezzlement. Flambard was also the first man to escape from the White Tower. His method of escape was simple: he gave his guards a barrel of wine. Once they were drunk, Ranulf climbed down from his cell on a rope smuggled to him by his friends.

DEFENSIVE DEVELOPMENTS

By the twelfth century the motte and bailey had become outmoded. Castles were now more elaborate affairs. They were built in durable stone, for while wood was a cheap material, it could easily be breached or set on fire. Castles now included a moat instead of a protective outer ditch, as well as an elaborate

gatehouse. This, the entrance to the castle, was its weakest part in the defense. To compensate for this, gatehouses were enlarged with projecting towers and a portcullis, a wooden grille reinforced with metal that could be lowered quickly to prevent entry into the castle. Murder holes were placed above the portcullis, allowing the defenders to hurl stones, arrows, and boiling oil onto the attacking force below.

The late twelfth century saw the introduction of the barbican. This was a rampart surmounted by a tower which, placed before the gatehouse, offered a first line of defense. The corners of castles were also protected with additional towers. The walls were intersected with arrow slits, giving archers an area from where they could defend the castle. By the early thirteenth century, castles no longer included a keep, instead the towers were enlarged, not only for protection, but also to provide a luxurious living space.

KRAK DES CHEVALIERS

The most advanced castles of the Middle Ages were built in the Holy Land. There, fortresses offered the Crusaders an effective means of holding on to the land without the need for maintaining large armies. Unlike European castles, Crusader castles were not built by local lords or sovereigns but by military orders such as the Knights Templar or Knights Hospitaller.

Krak des Chevaliers in Syria was one of the larger Crusader castles. Finished in 1170, it was designed as a concentric castle, meaning that it had two lines of concentric walls: an outer and an inner wall. Each was studded with towers, which protruded outwards enabling defenders to rain down arrows on the attacking force from three sides. The towers were semi-circular in design, which helped them deflect stones hurled at them by enemy catapults. The gateway had a "bent entrance,"

Above left and center: These views from Khotin Castle, Ukraine and Krak des Chevaliers in Syria show that the structures were sited where they would have a commanding view of the surrounding countryside.
Above right: From the outside the thick daunting walls and many arrow slots made strong castles look impregnable.

– a narrow passage which turned sharply. This served to hamper enemy attacks and impede the use of battering rams. Krak des Chevaliers also contained a large tower and accommodation for its 2000-strong garrison.

In its day, Krak des Chevaliers was regarded as impregnable. It was only captured once, after a siege lasting 34 days. Even then, the attacking Muslim army only managed to take the outer wall. The garrison took refuge behind the more powerful inner wall before surrendering with full honors.

It is believed that Krak des Chevaliers was modeled on the Theodosian Wall. This wall, built in the fourth century and named after the Byzantine emperor Theodosius, defended the city of Constantinople. Like Krak des Chevaliers, the Theodosian Wall had two parallel walls bristling with towers. In addition, it had a protective moat. Also, like the crusader castle, the Theodosian Wall was designed to be impregnable, and for more than 1,000 years it protected Constantinople from innumerable sieges.

THE WELSH MARCHES

The Theodosian Wall was also the inspiration for Caernarvon Castle, one of the most powerful castles ever built in Britain. In the late thirteenth century Wales rebelled against its English rulers. King Edward I crushed the rebellion ruthlessly and then imposed his sovereignty over the small Welsh state by building a series of castles in northern Wales. Caernarvon Castle, designed by James of Saint George, has only a single, powerful wall laid out in a figure of eight, intersected with ten octagonal towers. When it could only be accessed by passing over two drawbridges and was composed of five doors, six portcullises, and two towers.

The southern wall of Caernarvon Castle included firing galleries. These enabled archers to loose fire arrows from multiple directions to create what historian Allen Brown has called "one of the most formidable concentrations of fire-power to be found in the Middle Ages." Indeed, when Caernarvon Castle was besieged in 1404, it easily repelled a hostile army, despite being manned by a garrison only thirty-strong.

BRICKS

With the advent of large stone castles, building costs escalated. One way of keeping these costs down was by building castles out of brick. Brick was cheaper to produce and easier to transport than stone blocks. Brick castles were especially popular in Germany and Eastern Europe. The largest of these is Marienburg Castle, in present-day Prussia. It was completed in 1406 by the Teutonic Knights, a military order similar to the Templars and Hospitallers. The order had only just conquered Prussia and the vast castle was intended as a command center to control the area, as well as a base from which to launch further assaults into eastern Europe.

There are two gates on the outer wall, which are linked to the main castle by a drawbridge which spans a wide moat. The western part of the castle comprises a residence for the grand master of the order. This was later converted into a palace when the castle was captured by the Poles in 1457. The northern wing of Marienburg Castle held the arsenal, as well

From left to right: The boat-shaped Peñafiel Castle in Spain. Battlements or crenelations cut into the upper parapet gave protection to archers. Tomar Castle, Portugal: an example of buttresses that supported the main wall of castles. Chillon Castle, Switzerland. Parts of it date back to about 1005.

SIEGE WARFARE

As castles grew in complexity so did the weapons used to attack them. Up to the twelfth century, ballistas (similar to a giant crossbow) worked by using tension, and mangonels (catapults) were used to level castle walls. In the thirteenth century the trebuchet made its first appearance. This was a catapult powered by a counterweight that allowed stones as heavy as 33,100 pounds (15,000kg) to be projected up to a range of 984 feet (300m), often at a very high rate of fire.

Trebuchets were too big to transport, since some were up to fifty feet high. Instead they were built on site by teams of highly skilled carpenters, engineers, and blacksmiths. Needless to say, building trebuchets was a time-consuming and costly business. Many trebuchets had names: Phillip II of France built two for the siege of Acre, one called "God's Stone-Thrower" and the other "Bad Neighbor." At the siege of Stirling castle in 1304, King Edward I fielded a trebuchet named "Warwolf."

By the beginning of the fourteenth century, the first gunpowder weapons made their appearance. These weapons were small, cumbersome, and inaccurate. However, within a hundred years they had evolved into cannons, which, since they were smaller than a trebuchet, could be easily transported on wheeled gun-carriages. Because of gunpowder, cannons were infinitely more powerful than a trebuchet, certainly powerful enough to demolish a castle wall quickly. Against such a weapon, traditional castles were defenseless.

With the advent of gunpowder, castles were radically redesigned. Towers were removed, and walls were built with curved sides and packed with rubble and earth. This served to both absorb and deflect the impact of cannon balls. But despite these innovations, artillery spelt the end of the castle. By the end of the fifteenth century these magnificent homes became obsolete in terms of defense, but remained as symbols of power and luxury.

In the Middle Ages no man was more admired than the "perfect knight." Just as today most boys wish to be a professional footballer, most medieval boys would have wished to become a knight.

The medieval knight was above all a fighting machine. The most elite of all fighting men, the knight was clad from head to foot in armor, rode a huge war horse, and acted as the equivalent of a modern battle tank when he galloped into battle. No foot soldier could stand up to a knight, for even when unhorsed, he had the advantage of layers of heavy armor, as well as the best and most up-to-date weapons available at the time.

It was expensive being a knight: the specially trained fighting horses, armor, swords, and other weapons, and the upkeep of a squire were not cheap, but in return for his military service, the knight received a fief, or estate, from his liege lord if he had one. Also, by performing well at tournaments and "capturing" a wealthy knight or noble, high ransoms could be demanded and gained.

BECOMING A KNIGHT

THE PAGE

Most knights were the sons of noblemen who were bred to be warriors from a very young age. At around the age of eight, a boy from a noble family would be sent to the castle of a friend or relative to be trained as a page, learning courtly manners while waiting upon the lord and lady and their household. He would also learn about the usefulness of allegiances with other noble families and pick up the politics of the day by listening carefully to what was being said around him.

As well as manners, the boy would learn to wrestle, ride a horse, use a spear, sword and shield, and the basic tactics of other weapons, and begin to joust against a wooden target. A particular exercise was to ride against the quintain, a dummy target filled with sand that would swing round and buffet the rider if it was not struck cleanly. Prospective knights also learnt the rudiments of arithmetic and reading and writing, especially Latin, which was

Top: Knights relied on their warhorses, so they made sure that the animals were also armored.

Above: When jousting or in battle, knights aimed their lances between the joints of their opponent's armor.

Left: The lengthy process of dressing a knight in his full armor.

the language of learning in the Middle Ages of western Europe (together with Norman French), although many would fail to master it.

However "book learning" was not essential for a knight: after all, he would be expected to hire a clerk or scribe to do that sort of work for him. Clerks (or clerics) were educated by the Church, being often lay priests attached to a noble household. Many were bastard sons of the nobles they served, so their loyalty to their fathers was total as they relied on them for their status in the family. They were generally fluent in Latin, the "official" language of the day, and could write legal documents and letters for their lord and keep household accounts. Joining the Church was sometimes the only path for the younger sons of nobles and less wealthy familes, and in addition, many boys were not cut out to be warriors and so personally chose to join the Church, their families paying for this privilege.

THE SQUIRE

By the time he was 15 or 16 years old, a page boy became a squire in service to a knight. His duties now included dressing the knight in the morning, serving all of his lord's meals, caring for the knight's horse and weapons, and cleaning and repairing the armor by hammering out dents (serious damage would be repaired by a smith or specialist armorer). He followed the knight to tournaments, learned the heraldic arms and who were the friends and associates of other knights and nobles there, and assisted his lord on the battlefield. A squire also prepared himself by learning how to handle a sword and lance while wearing 40 lbs (18.14 k) of armor and riding a horse.

THE KNIGHT

When he was about 20 years old, a squire could become a knight after proving himself worthy. The initiation of a boy into a warrior was originally quite simple: the sword was consecrated, the oath taken, the blow delivered. By the tenth century the ceremony had been richly elaborated by the Christians. Away from the battlefields where knighthoods were given quickly and with little ceremony, a typical investiture had several stages.

The candidate fasted and abstained from sex. His sword, shield, lance, and banner were blessed, but not the spurs, which were regarded as a secular gift given for an act of valor (the old

A TYPICAL OATH FOR A KNIGHT

I here swear fealty and do homage to the Crown of ... to ever be a good knight and true, reverent and generous, shield of the weak, obedient to my liege lord, foremost in battle, courteous at all times, champion of the right and the good of existence. Thus swear I ....

Above: A dubbing ceremony.

term "earned his spurs" comes from this). The church would accept the candidate on the evening before the ceremony. After being ritually bathed, he would spend the night in the church alone in prayer and thought. After confession he would go to mass, followed by the ritual of knighthood, which would take place in the presence of family, friends, and nobility. Here is the ceremony from the Pontifical of Bishop Guillaume Durand of Mende in the thirteenth century:

Taking up the naked sword and laying it upon the altar, he says "Bless this sword, that Thy servant may henceforth defend churches, widows, orphans, and all those who serve God, against the cruelty of heretics and infidels. Bless this sword Holy Lord, Almighty Father, Eternal God. Bless it in the name of the coming of Christ and by the gift of the Holy Ghost the Comforter. And may Thy servant, armed with Thy love, tread all his visible enemies underfoot, and, master of victory, rest forever protected from all attack."

A prayer from the Old Testament is then read: "Blessed be the Lord God who formed my hands for battle and my fingers for war. He is my salvation, He is my refuge, He setteth me free." In the name of the Trinity, the Bishop then places the sword in the right hand of the knight, receives it back, delivers the "blow," and girds the sword in its scabbard around the waist of the kneeling man, who then brandishes the sword three times around his head before placing it back in the scabbard. The Bishop gives the "kiss of peace" and says "Be a soldier peaceful, courageous, faithful, and devoted to God."

DUBBING

The Christian rites of knighthood, parts of which are still in use today all over Europe, originate from the pagan Teutonic tribes. The term "dubbing," a blow, is from the German meaning "to strike."

The squire knelt in front of a lord, who tapped the squire lightly on each shoulder with his sword, and proclaimed him a knight. This was symbolic of what occurred in the early middle ages where the person doing the dubbing would actually hit the squire forcefully, knocking him over. The Germanic rite included a strike or a cut to the neck, which was symbolic of the last hit the new knight should accept without responding. It was a test of strength and a reminder of the seriousness of the oath taken. After the dubbing, a great feast followed with music and dancing.

THE ORIGINS OF HERALDRY

A soldier in all his protective gear would be unrecognizable to others in the chaos of a battlefield. This became an important issue during the first Crusade in the eleventh century when nobles and their followers from one area found themselves beside thousands of others from many parts of Europe: each fighting faction needed to keep in contact with its countrymen.

So began heraldry – the use of personal coats of arms or distinctive designs and colors on a "surcoat" or tunic worn over chain mail or other protection, together with banners, shields, and horsecloth, all marking out who was who. A famous example is, of course, the Knights Templar with their long, white cloth tunics displaying a large red cross on the breast and back.

Originally, heraldic arms were personal: members of the same family would have quite different arms from each other.

But, over time, prominent families began to keep certain coats of arms that were then passed down to the next generation.

By the mid-thirteenth century heraldry, with all its emerging rules and regulations, was beginning to be well established all over Europe. From this developed a strong growing sense of national identity, with realms and kingdoms adopting specific coats of arms, together with their army units, many of which are still in use today.

In heraldry, the hilt of a sword often has three circles around it meaning: Good Thought, Good Deed, and Good Word.

THE ROLE OF MARSHALS AND HERALDS

Arguments often arose over coats of arms and so authority was given to the marshals to handle disputes. Heralds assisted the marshals with these disputes, recorded genealogies, and also helped organize public ceremonies and tournaments.

TOURNAMENTS AND JOUSTING

The tourney became a very social and exciting occasion for all, no matter what status they were. Everyone from peasants

This reenactment scene shows how heraldic symbols were proudly displayed on horses and banners, as well as on knights' surcoats.

to royalty loved to attend and enjoy the action. Pedlars and merchants sold their wares, musicians played, bets were placed, and young women and noble ladies eyed the knights, picking out favorites and hoping to be noticed and admired.

This was the place for a young knight to show off his fighting skills, get experience and get noticed. Plus, with luck, he could defeat a wealthy knight, confiscate his horse and expensive armor, and perhaps even ransom him for a high price.

No one knows for sure when the first tournaments began, as martial games and exercises are very old, but by the end of the eleventh century it had developed more or less into a formal style with spectators. This may have been so that knights could practise the new ways of fighting on horseback – especially using the "couched" lance charge – galloping down the list towards an opponent and attempting to unseat him (jousting). The list was constructed on level ground, with barriers down the sides and a low fence in the middle to prevent the knights on horseback from colliding with each other and to keep them on a straight course; several were usually constructed for a tourney. To encourage archery skills, tournaments would also organize competitions with prizes for the winners.

As well as the individual contests, a tourney usually involved two teams formed to fight against each other; heralds and marshals

often had to be careful who took part in which team to avoid excessive bloodshed. After the staged battle, which often covered several acres of by then destroyed land, the knights would round up their bruised captives and take them back to their camp to arrange ransoms. Many knights such as William Marshal made their fame and fortune from taking part in tourneys.

There were generally three different types of tourney with various weapons and rules of combat.

- The "mêlée" was fought between two teams of knights in open fields or in the lists.
- The individual joust.
- The practice tournament where the rules and ceremonies were more relaxed. The quintain was used, as well as a ring suspended from a rope which the knight had to get on the tip of his lance (these practices are still used in Italy).

Tournaments were common all over Europe, but especially in England, France, Germany, Italy, and the Low Countries, and not all of them were considered as games. The name comes from the Spanish "torneo," a "hostile maneuver," and many personal feuds were worked out in tourneys, since open hostilities elsewhere would not have been allowed by the rulers.

The pageantry of tourneys, with their ceremonies and rules, slowly transformed the brutality of earlier tourneys into chivalric entertainment.

Above: The heat and press of a mêlée.
Below: The shock of a mounted knight charging foot soldiers.

Generally, only knights were allowed to take part in a tournament (except for archery contests). In Germany, however, there is evidence that adulterous knights were banned from taking part, and contestants without knightly status were also permitted. German knights also favored the use of the mace which was not often used elsewhere.

In 1240, around 60 to 80 contestants were killed at one particular tourney in Cologne, reported the French chronicler Jean Froissart.

The Church did not approve of tourneys, which they considered to be the continuation of dangerous "pagan games" that caused the deaths of young men. At the Council of Clermont in 1130, Pope Innocent II forbade tourneys, and the Council would not allow church burials for men killed in them.

Henry II of England banned them, and Philip Augustus of France made his sons take an oath not to take part. When King John of England died, his young heir Henry III was a minor, and the English kingdom came under the regency of William Marshal. Tourneying was forbidden during most of this time in case it incited political unrest (the barons forcing the Magna Carta on John was still fresh in many minds). Nobles who violated this ban (and there were several) were severely punished and their lands confiscated. The ban was lifted, in part, when Henry came to the throne.

Above left and right: All the horrors of combat.
Right: Women enjoyed the opportunity to watch their favorite knights jousting.

SOME FAMOUS KNIGHTS

JOAN OF ARC (THE MAID OF ORLÉANS/ JEANNE D'ARC) (C.1412–31)

Joan achieved the status of being one of the great heroic knights. She was born into an ordinary peasant family from Domremy, on the edge of Champagne and Lorraine, when France was in the middle of the Hundred Years' War with England. She had no formal education except in the doctrines of the Church. From an early age she showed a desire for devotional meditation, going into trances, experiencing angelic visions, and hearing "voices." One of the visions she experienced was of St. Michael who told her she must go to help the French royal heir Charles (VII).

Persuading military leaders, and dressed in men's clothes, she was helped to travel to and gain an audience with Charles. After being examined for heresy, Joan convinced Charles and his aides of the truth of her vision, and was given troops. In 1429 she and her army defeated the English at Orléans and Patay, which led to Charles being crowned at Reims Cathedral

in her presence. She was captured later by the Burgundians at Compière and sold to the English.

Being female did her no favors at the court of the inquisition at Rouen where she was tried for sorcery and blasphemy. Wearing men's clothes and cutting her hair short also marked her out as being too strange. Burned at the stake in 1431, she was made a saint in 1920.

WILLIAM MARSHAL (C. 1147–1219)

Famous in his day, the English knight William Marshal was an intelligent and outstanding warrior, tactician, politician, and courtier. His father, John Marshal, a minor baron, was an royal master-marshal at Henry I of England's court. Although not of royal blood, William experienced royal politics at the early age

Left: A stained glass portrait of Joan of Arc.
Right: The unusual round Temple Church in London that contains the supposed effigy of William Marshal.

of around five when he was held for at least a year as a hostage by King Stephen during the civil war between Stephen and Mathilda, the only surviving child of Henry I.

He made his reputation, and a great deal of wealth, fighting in tourneys. Once, when he didn't turn up to collect his prize, he was found with his head on an anvil, the smith bashing his helmet into shape so it could come off.

He became Lord of Striguel when he married the heiress, Isabel, in 1189. From then on, lands and castles in England, the Welsh Marches and Ireland came under his jurisdiction. A loyal royalist, he stood by and advised King John of England when the barons forced him to sign the Magna Carta. When John died in 1213 and his heir, Henry III, was too young to take the throne, William was appointed Regnum Regis (Regent) of England. His effigy lies on the floor of the round Templar Church, off Fleet Street, London.

ULRICH VON LIECHTENSTEIN (1200–78)

Ulrich von Liechtenstein, from Murau in present-day Austria, was a nobleman, knight, politician, and minnessanger (minstrel). He was fortunate to have had the classic knightly training from page to squire to knight, being "dubbed" by Duke Leopold VI in 1223. Leader of the Duchy of Styria's nobility, he took part in its absorption into the Habsburg empire, and become its governor (in modern terms, Styria was south of Austria and north of Slovenia).

He became famous not only for his specially made helmet displaying the Roman goddess of love, Venus, but also for his altruistic and chivalric poetry. *Frauendienst* (*Service of the Lady*), supposedly autobiographical, was completed in 1255. It tells of the romantic quest of a knight determined to obtain, with great honor and deeds, the love of noble women. In 1257 he wrote *Frauenbuch*, a poem regretting the gradual loss of chivalry and courtship in that day and age.

Liechtenstein's name became well known in modern times thanks to the 2001 film *A Knight's*

Ulrich von Liechenstein wearing his famous helmet showing the goddess Venus.

Tale, when the hero pretends to be a knight and takes on Ulrich's name.

ROBIN HOOD: A LEGENDARY KNIGHT

Known in English medieval folk culture and later poems and ballads, the legend of Robin Hood changed dramatically over time. The basis of the story is always the same: Robin was an outlaw dressed in green, who lived in the wild woods, was a highly skilled archer, and robbed from the rich to give to the poor.

However several early records point to him living in Yorkshire, not the Sherwood Forest of Nottinghamshire with which he is now associated. Also, many accounts now have him as the dispossessed knight the Earl of Huntingdon, who supported King Richard the Lionheart and was driven to become an outlaw by Richard's brother King John. However, most early sources hint that he was a commoner, a yeoman, meaning that he was not a peasant but was not noble by any means.

His men Little John, Will Scarlet, and Much the Miller's Son soon became part of the legend, as did Robin's conflicts with the Sheriff of Nottingham. Friar Tuck and the love-interest, Maid Marion, were later added to the story. The many, many tales of Robin Hood's exploits and adventures show that a folk-hero can remain popular for centuries.

Robin Hood practicing archery with his Merry Men.

ARMOR AND OTHER PROTECTIVE CLOTHING

Thick, boiled leather was the earliest form of protection around vulnerable parts of the body. Later, metal studs, rings, or other pieces were stitched onto the leather. Chain or ring mail was introduced as early as the third century BCE. It was expensive to produce (sometimes even more so than plate) and was prized highly by fighting men, often being worn under plate as secondary protection.

Plate armor started to replace chain mail from about 1275 CE onwards and, by 1325, very efficient armor plate was made, although mail was still used.

Armor for the war horse should not be forgotten; it was just as important for a mounted soldier to kit out his expensive and expensively trained horse as himself.

THE BLACKSMITH

Blacksmiths and armorers were a vital part of any army. If captured, they were rarely killed, their skills being far too important to lose.

THE AX

An ancient weapon whose design was often adapted and used continuously throughout medieval Europe. The Saxons were very adept in its use.

THE POLEAX

A longer, shafted ax used by foot soldiers. It also had a blade or hammer on one side with a spike or blade on the top of the shaft.

THE BILL

A common weapon for foot soldiers from the mid-thirteenth century onwards. The head on the shaft was made of iron, with a long, single cutting edge that divided into a curving "bill" and a spike, with another shorter spike on the back.

THE GISARME

Used from the twelfth to the mid-fifteenth centuries, it had a curved half-moon blade with the cutting edge on the outer curve.

THE GLAIVE

Mainly used in France and Germany. It had a single-edged blade with a double edge on part of the back. Some had additional blades, spurs or hooks on the top edge, which was blunt.

THE HALBARD

First in Switzerland in the thirteenth century, it was similar to the poleax with an ax blade accompanied by a spike on the other side of the shaft.

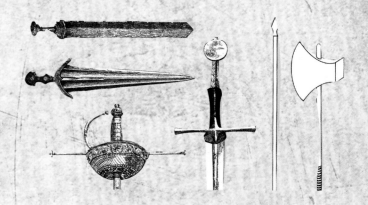

Above: A selection of medieval weapons.
Below: (first, second, third) Great helms, also known as Crusader helms or pot helms were hot, heavy, and obscured the vision; (fourth) helm and chain mail; (fifth and sixth) By the late 1300s most men were wearing hinged bascinet helmets, often with a pointed "pig face."

THE MACE

An ancient, heavy, club-type weapon that was continually adapted. The head could be made of stone or metal, and was shaped to give better penetration against armor. Around 27.5–35.5 inches long (70–90 cms) for foot soldiers, longer if fighting on horseback.

THE PARTISAN

In use from the mid-fourteenth century. The triangular blade evolved into a tapering blade with its shoulders curved up into hooks. It was easy to use and inflicted devastating wounds.

THE QUARTER STAFF

An ancient weapon romanticized by tales about Robin Hood, the quarter staff was very useful at close-quarter fighting, even against a sword, but not against the spear or pike. Traditionally its length was from middle fingertip to middle fingertip with arms outstretched. Preferably a matured, hard wood such as oak or elm, it was essentially a weapon of peasants and was used against marauding armies.

THE SPEAR, LANCE, AND PIKE

These were the main weapons for the foot soldier and were similar in construction, having a sharp, leaf-shaped metal tip, or a rounded spike on top of a long shaft.

THE COUCHED LANCE

The couched lance, where a heavier than usual lance was tucked securely under the right arm by each mounted warrior who would then charge as a group at the enemy, was a new and very effective Norman fighting tactic at the end of the eleventh

A simple wooden crossbow.
Below: The ball and chain, also known as a flail.

century. It required great skill to use and jousting exercises became very popular.

THE SWORD

It is impossible to say exactly when the sword was developed. Simply by widening and lengthening a spear head, then adding a better grip, we have a sword.

By the fifth century various parts of Europe had developed reasonable methods of sword production – the key was not just the design: it was the quality of the metal, how the ore was smelted and the blade forged.

The Vikings had considerable skills, involving complex methods of twisting strips of iron together, and repeatedly heating and hammering until the blade was forged. The Saxon sword was similar, but lighter and less strong than the Vikings, and Saxons also had a back-up, all-purpose dagger called the scramasax or seax.

There was little change in the general fighting sword until the arrival of armor plate. When plate began to replace chain mail, new sword types had to evolve to cope. The lighter cutting blades were gradually replaced by heavier, longer, and more sharply pointed ones to pierce the plate, and the grip was lengthened. Obviously, combat techniques had to be adapted depending on the gear of the opponent.

The "classic" two-handed longsword, and its subtype, the hand-and-a-half (where the pommel was held), was used throughout Europe from the late medieval period (late thirteenth century) until the early Renaissance (sixteenth century). While rich or well-connected soldiers most certainly kept up-to-date with the latest trends in weapons, in general a huge collection of types was used in conflict. Any sword was better than nothing!

For the foot soldier the sword was a secondary weapon to the spear, lance, or long pike, and was used in close-quarter fighting where a spear or pike was unsuitable or would injure

Left: Hand-to-hand fighting in defense of a castle.

comrades. The double-handed sword was preferred over the usual one, or one-and-a-half grip of the mounted soldier.

THE LONGBOW

Developed from the ancient, shorter hunting bow which had less range, the longbow, standing about 6 foot high (1.83 meters), became one of the most important weapons for the medieval army - a skilled archer could kill an enemy 400 yards (366 meters) away. It was in use from the twelfth century.

Bows were generally made from yew wood which is strong yet very flexible. Strings were made from the intestines, sinew, or hair of animals, and even linen or hemp treated with beeswax.

If an archer was captured, it was common practice to cut off his first and middle fingers so he could not pull a bow again. So archers would wave to each other across the battlefield to show that they still had their fingers and could

shoot. This has given us the two-fingered "V" gesture which still survives today!

It took years of training and great strength to become a good archer. In medieval England every fit and able-bodied boy and man had to practice the bow after Sunday church service. Church towers were the perfect target and many still bear the scars.

THE CROSSBOW

More expensive to construct than the longbow, and easier to use but slower to fire, the crossbow became a common castle defense weapon as it did not take long to master, unlike the longbow. A bolt (or quarrel) could pierce armor.

BATTERING RAMS AND SIEGE MACHINES

In many old movies a castle's big doors are attacked by a huge tree trunk, the original and basic battering ram. This was a highly effective weapon, but was countered when the defenders poured boiling oil on the attackers. In response, protective wooden coverings were developed with the tree trunk suspended on ropes from stout beams.

CATAPULTS

Most catapults were counter-weighted with a rope and pulley system, and worked on wheels for ease of use.

THE MANGONEL

Threw projectiles such as large rocks or firepots from a bucket. Dead human bodies, heads, and animals were also thrown to demoralize and spread disease.

THE ONAGER

Threw projectiles from a sling, so was not as effective as the mangonel.

THE SPRINGALD

Used from the late twelfth to early thirteenth centuries. It was based on the crossbow and Greek ballista but with arms swinging inwards. It threw large bolts and sometimes Greek Fire (an incendiary weapon – composition now unknown).

THE TREBUCHET

Used from the twelfth to the fifteenth centuries, the trebuchet was a massive siege catapult that could throw projectiles weighing up to 350 pounds (140 k) at great speed. Powered by gravity, it rotated a throwing arm 4 to 6 times the length of the counterweight arm; the sling at the end of the arm also increased the speed of the projectiles.

FIREARMS

Gunpowder was known in Europe by the fourteenth century and primitive cannons were experimented with, usually with devastating effect as the cannon would often burst with the shock, which must have terrifying and dangerous for the soldiers commanding them. It was not until the very late fifteenth century onwards that more stable firearms came into general use.

The first English cannons were built around 1327, and were used at the siege of Calais and the Battle of Crécy in 1346 during

Left: The use of scaling ladders in a siege.
Right: The mounted knights in this image must have been stifling in their full armor, covered by surcoats, and with full-head helmets.

the Hundred Years War. They were few in number and their effectiveness doubtful.

The earliest known illustration of a European cannon is in the English *Milemete Manuscript* of 1326, and in records in Florence. The earliest known surviving firearm, dating to about 1396, is in Estonia.

CAVALRY VS. FOOT SOLDIERS

History recalls only one instance of infantry beating mounted cavalry, a consequence of the Battle of Hastings in England in 1066. There, the Saxon King Harold's personal guard of house carls, fighting on foot, were beaten by the Norman invaders who were on horseback. Most of the surviving carls left England after Harold's death.

Later, in 1081, at Durazzo on the Adriatic coast, the Normans were fighting the Byzantine Emperor's forces that contained several mercenary groups. One of these groups, the elite Varangian Guard, which included many angry Saxon veterans from the Battle of Hastings, attacked so fiercely with their battle axes that the horses bolted and the Norman knights were driven into the sea.

But the enthusiastic Saxons were cut off from their supporting forces, and Norman spear- and crossbow-men were rallied by Sikelgaita, Duchess of Guiscard, and they killed most of the Guard. The survivors ran into a church and were burnt to death when the Normans set fire to it.

Norman cavalry fight Saxon footmen at the Battle of Hastings.

HOLY WAR: THE CRUSADES AND THE MILITARY RELIGIOUS ORDERS

Sacred to the three Abrahamic religions of Judaism, Christianity, and Islam, Jerusalem was a center of contention between the different cultures of Christian Europe and the Muslim world.

Although Muslim Arab armies had taken control of Palestine in around 600, for many centuries Christian pilgrims were still able to visit Jerusalem and other sites in the "Holy Land." But in 1095 the Seljuk Turks, who were expanding their dominion in the Middle East, banned Christians and Jews from entering Jerusalem, and began to threaten the Byzantine empire's holdings in the region.

In 1095 Byzantine Emperor Alexios I Komnenos sent for help to Pope Urban II. In response, the pope called for a volunteer army to capture Jerusalem, and set in motion hundreds of years of holy war.

The word "crusade" comes from a French term meaning to "take the cross," since the volunteers were supposed to receive a cross from the pope or his representatives and to wear a cross badge as a symbol of becoming a soldier of the church. Pope Urban called for both rich and poor to become Crusaders, and as well as appealing to men's sense of piety, he also offered a

Some of the main routes European fighters followed to reach the Holy Land, either by land or sea.

very practical inducement in the form of absolution for all sins: Crusaders would go straight to heaven after their death.

THE FIRST CRUSADE

Although there was an earlier "People's Crusade" led by Peter the Hermit, the official First Crusade was launched in 1096. Mainly composed of French and Norman knights and soldiers, the expedition took the best part of two years to reach its destination. The Crusaders reclaimed several former Byzantine

Left: Stained glass window of the Crusader king Louis IX of France.
Right: Images of the First Crusade: martyrdom at the hands of the Turks; entry into Jerusalem.

Left: The Second Crusade.
Right: Embarking for the Holy Land, the Crusaders proudly displayed their personal banners. The fleets that carried troops across the Mediterranean grew wealthy on the trade.

territories in Anatolia from the Turks, and succeeded in capturing Antioch in 1098 and Jerusalem in 1099. The city was ransacked by the Crusaders and its inhabitants – Muslim, Jewish, or Christian – were massacred.

From a military viewpoint the First Crusade was a resounding success. The Crusaders, called "Franks" by the Turks since so many were from France, established four Crusader states in Syria and Palestine: the Kingdom of Jerusalem, the County of Tripoli, the Principality of Antioch, and the County of Edessa. Pilgrimage routes were re-opened and the great military monastic orders of the Knights Templar and the Knights Hospitaller were formed to protect and serve pilgrims.

THE SECOND CRUSADE

But success was short-lived. Not even fifty years later, the Muslims rallied and retook Edessa, prompting calls for a Second Crusade. This expedition, from 1147–9, failed to achieve any lasting victories, however en route to the Holy Land a detachment of Crusaders taking the western route through Europe helped the Portuguese wrest Lisbon from the Arab conquerors of Iberia.

THE THIRD CRUSADE

Christian Europe was shocked in 1187 when the Turkish leader Saladin destroyed the "Frankish" army at the battle of Hattin and went on to capture Jerusalem as well as most of the Crusader territories. A cultured, chivalrous soldier who was respected by his European enemies, Saladin ensured that the inhabitants of Jerusalem were not molested, that the priests could leave safely, and that buildings were left intact.

The Third Crusade was launched in 1189. Three separate armies, led by three of Europe's greatest rulers, set out for the Holy Land. The 70-year-old Holy Roman Emperor Frederick (Friedrich) Barbarossa drowned en route, and his disheartened German army mainly returned home. This left the rivals Richard I of England (the Lionheart) and Philip II Augustus of France in charge. Their alliance did not last long. The two armies took the town of Acre on the coast of what is now Israel, then the French king returned home. Richard stayed but never achieved his aim of recapturing Jerusalem. When he returned to Europe

Below: The citadel of David became the seat of the Crusader kings, but the sight of the Dome of the Rock, a sacred site for Muslims, would have been a daily reminder of why the Saracens wanted the city back.

in 1192, the Crusaders had control of only a narrow strip of coastline in Syria and Palestine, but he and Saladin had agreed that Christian pilgrims could enter Jerusalem freely.

THE FOURTH CRUSADE

This crusade originally intended to reclaim the Holy Land by attacking through Egypt. Gathering at Venice in 1201, the army was persuaded by the Venetians to instead attack Constantinople, sacking the city in 1204. The Venetians had prepared a huge fleet for the expedition, expecting to transport many more soldiers than the number who turned up. So, in order to recoup their expenses and to settle old grudges, they convinced the Fourth Crusade to support their preferred rival for the Byzantine throne. Although excommunicated by the horrified pope, Innocent III, when the would-be Crusaders returned home and gave part of their loot to the church, they were welcomed back into the fold.

THE LATER CRUSADES

1212 saw the disastrous Children's Crusade, in which French and German children followed a call from a young preacher to make their way to Jerusalem, where they believed God would reward their innocence by forcing the Turks to cede the city. The children died in their thousands from starvation or cold, and most of those who did manage to reach the Middle East ended up enslaved.

The Fifth Crusade of 1213–21, which failed to win any territory from the Muslims,

Above left: A 16th-century depiction of the Crusader sack of Constantinople.
Above right: The four Crusader states in Palestine and Syria.
Below: A Crusader and a Saracen playing chess. There were periods of peace and truce.

was the last to be called by a pope. Later crusades were organized by individual monarchs, such as Holy Roman Emperor Frederick II who went on the Sixth Crusade in 1228. He fought no battles, instead negotiating for a short-lived Christian rule of Jerusalem. Louis IX of France (St. Louis) organized the Seventh Crusade from 1248 to 1254, a disaster that saw him captured and held to ransom. Despite this misadventure, Louis returned on crusade in 1270, only to die from disease with many of his men. This was the last major attempt by Europeans to retake the Holy Land. Other expeditions did follow, but in 1291 the last Christian stronghold of Acre was taken by the Turks and the period of the crusades came to an end.

EUROPEAN CRUSADES

Holy wars were called by popes not only against Muslim Turks. Christian heretics and European pagans were also subjected to crusades, for example the Albigensian Crusade in 1209–29 and the Northern Crusades carried out by the Teutonic Knights against Slavs and other non-Christians in eastern Europe.

THE IMPACT OF THE CRUSADES

Crusader knights returning to Europe brought many innovations with them, from baths and carpets to exotic foodstuffs, sparking a new desire for a trade in luxury goods. They also brought back new ideas in science and philosophy. While Europe had grown disorganized and backwards in the Early Middle Ages, the Islamic world had become civilized and sophisticated, and Arabs had not only preserved knowledge from ancient Greece and Rome, but had also experimented and developed new scientific knowledge. The meeting of Christian and Muslim worlds was a true culture clash. It also left a lasting legacy of hatred towards Christian Holy Warriors in many parts of the Middle East.

RICHARD THE LIONHEART (1157–99)

The son of Henry II, Richard inherited not only England but also most of Wales as well as lands in Anjou, Normandy, Gasgony, and other parts of France through his mother Eleanor of Aquitaine. He much preferred his French holdings: during his ten-year reign as king of England he spent only one year in the country.

In 1190 Richard joined the Third Crusade. Already famous, his incisive exploits compared to the vacillations of many other Crusading leaders made him a Christian superstar. Although he never met the Muslim leader Saladin, the two exchanged correspondence and gifts, and respected each other as true, noble warriors.

Richard never achieved his goal of reclaiming Jerusalem, and on his return from Crusade in 1192 he was captured by enemies and eventually held to ransom by Heinrich VI, the Holy Roman Emperor. Two years later he was released after a massive ransom was paid. According to legend, Richard's minstrel, Blondel, discovered his place of captivity by singing outside various castles. An advocate of the new weapon, the crossbow, Richard was killed by a crossbow bolt while assaulting the castle of Chalus in France.

SALADIN (1138–93)

Salah ad-Din Yusuf al-Ayyoub, known in English as Saladin, is one of the greatest historical heroes of the Arab world. A Kurd, he took military service under the Seljuk Turks then founded his own Ayyubid dynasty based in Egypt. He had a major impact on the development of the city of Cairo.

Saladin was a natural military leader and tactician. He expanded his sultanate into Yemen and parts of Syria, and began a

Above: Richard the Lionheart.
Right: Saladin, the great Turkish leader.

campaign against the Franks in 1182, inflicting a shattering defeat upon the Crusader kingdom and capturing Jerusalem in 1187.

Saladin was respected not just for his military skill but also for his sense of chivalry and honor. He even offered his own doctor to Richard the Lionheart when the king was wounded.

Saladin survived two attempts on his life by the Assassins, the terrifying Ismaili Shia sect whose members were accredited with an almost magical ability to infiltrate even heavily guarded palaces. Having pushed the Crusaders out of almost all of Palestine, Saladin died in Damascus after a short illness.

THE MILITARY RELIGIOUS ORDERS

The major military orders were initiated by the impact of the Crusades; by the Moorish invasion of Iberia, southern France, and various countries in the Mediterranean; and pagan European tribes that refused to convert to Christianity. Permanent army-style "garrisons" were not common in medieval Europe, so the appeal of these emerging orders was twofold: the stability of a monastic institution together with a military background enabling them to protect fellow Christians.

After the First Crusade in 1099, Christian pilgrims from all over Europe flocked to the Holy Land to visit Jerusalem. Although Jerusalem was safe, much of Europe and the Middle East was filled with roving bandits and was very dangerous for travelers. The great military orders provided security and protection.

THE THREE MAIN ORDERS

THE KNIGHTS TEMPLARS (THE ORDER OF THE POOR KNIGHTS OF THE TEMPLE OF SOLOMON)

Founded: Discussed around 1113–15, and formed after Easter 1119 to defend pilgrims. Hughes de Payen is believed to have been "magister templi" (the Grand Master) in 1125. Endorsed by the pope at the Council of Troyes in 1129. It took a further 20 years before the Order had a working hierarchy, with Rules of conduct and discipline based on religious structures, and the money to operate effectively. A Papal Bull of 1139 exempted the Order from paying taxes and obeying local laws.

Symbol: From 1147, the red cross on white. Their emblem was two knights mounted on one horse, showing the individual poverty of the members.

Membership: Around 15–20,000 at its peak, but only about 10 percent were combatants. Mainly from English, French, German, and Scottish noble families.

In the 1130s, with the financial support of St. Bernard of Clairvaux and other wealthy benefactors, the Order became popular all over Christendom and grew very fast with many sons of the nobility keen to join and help. They took part in key battles and their reputation and prestige grew.

WEALTH

About 1150 the Templars devised one of the first banking systems to help prevent bandits and thieves targeting Christian pilgrims or crusaders on their way to Jerusalem. For a small fee, pilgrims could deposit their valuables at a local Templar preceptory in return for a letter of credit (similar to a check). Pilgrims could then hand the letter in to any of the other Templar preceptories across Europe and the Holy Land and get their money back. The Order became very rich and influential, owning lands and properties all over Europe and the Near East, and lending vast sums to royalty and nobles.

DOWNFALL

In the early 1300s a knight who had been expelled from the Order started rumors that the Templars were heretical and conducted obscene rituals. King Philip IV of France, who was greatly in debt to them, grabbed this chance to avoid having to repay the Templars. He convinced the Church to take action on the suspicion of blasphemy, and, on Friday 13th October, 1307 his troops arrested many Templars, including the Grand Master, Jacques de Molay (this is the origin of the superstition regarding Friday the thirteenth). The Pope's Decree banning the Order followed in 1312 with many Templar properties passing to the Knights Hospitaller. However, some countries considered the Templars innocent and refused to arrest them or confiscate their lands. Although in France the knights were tortured until they confessed to blasphemy and were subsequently exectured, in other countries very few were convicted. For example, in Aragon and Castile all Templars were found innocent. Many Templars fled to England, Germany, and Scotland, or joined the Teutonic Knights or Knights Hospitaller.

Hugo of Gumbach, Templar Master of Germany, decided to take things into his own hands. Selecting 20 of his best knights, he marched with them in full armor into a council meeting convened by the Bishop of Metz to discuss the Templars.

Firmly stating that the Order was innocent and that the Pope was "evil and should be deposed," he added that all his men were willing to undertake trial by combat against the council members. After a stunned silence the Templar issue was immediately abandoned!

The Templars left many mysteries. Philip of France hoped to seize their wealth, but he was thwarted. Perhaps warned by sympathizers, the Templars moved their treasure out of France, and it has never yet been found. The Templar naval fleet, then the greatest in the world, also escaped capture, and according to some legends the piratical emblem of the skull and crossbones derives from their new ventures. In addition, sculptures of maize in Rosslyn Chapel, Scotland suggest that the Templars crossed the Atlantic and landed in America. Although the order was destroyed, its legends still live on.

THE KNIGHTS HOSPITALLER (THE KNIGHTS OF RHODES)

Founded: Several years before the First Crusade in 1099 as a non-military hospice, at the Hospital of St John of Jerusalem, for pilgrims visiting Jerusalem. Considered the second greatest religious knightly order. A Papul Bull was granted in 1113.

Membership: Several thousands at its peak; mainly from England and Italy, but also the sons of noble families from France, Portugal, and Spain; nuns were also affiliated with the order.

Symbol: White cross on dark brown/black.

THE TEUTONIC KNIGHTS (ORDER OF THE BROTHERS OF THE GERMAN HOUSE OF ST. MARY IN JERUSALEM)

Founded: In a beached boat in Acre, originally as a hospital for injured German knights. Confirmed by the Pope in 1191. Considered the third major religious order of knights during the Crusader period.

Symbol: Black cross on white.

Membership: Although the Teutonic Knights accepted those who had not been knighted, they followed similar precepts to other religious knightly orders, especially the Knights Templar and Knights Hospitaller.

Reconstruction of the outfit a member of the Teutonic Order might have worn.

Other knightly orders joined the Teutonic Knights, bringing their membership to over 2,000 by 1279: the Livonian Knights (Brothers of the Sword), and the Prussian Order of Dobryzeń.

When granted trading rights by the pope, their outlook became more political and commercial. They suffered a great defeat against the Poles in 1410 at Tannenburg and in 1466 came under Polish authority. Later, when Prussia was secularized by their Grand Master, Albert of Brandenburg, the Teutonic Knights lost most of their power.

OTHER ORDERS

Order of St. Lazarus
Founded: Late eleventh century by members of the Knights Hospitaller who had leprosy to aid those suffering from the disease. One of the oldest orders.

ENGLAND

Hospitallers of St. Thomas of Canterbury at Acre
Founded: 1191 for the care of the sick and dying, and for the burial of Christian knights. Membership was for the English only.

GERMANY

Order of the Livonian Brothers of the Sword
Founded: 1202 by the Bishop of Riga. Confirmed by the pope 1204. Comprised of German fighting monks, it merged with the Teutonic Knights as the Livonian Order branch in 1236.

HUNGARY

Order of the Dragon
Founded: 1408 by Sigismund, King of Hungary (later the Holy Roman Emperor). Popular in Germany and Italy, the Order played a crucial role against the Ottoman invasions in Hungary, Serbia, and Wallachia. The father of the legendary Dracula was a member, giving him the name "Dracul."

ITALY

Order of St. James of Altopascio
Founded: 1070–80 by Matilda of Canossa in Tuscany for pilgrims traveling to Rome and the Holy Land. Merged with the Order of Our Lady of Bethlehem in 1459.

SPAIN

The Knights of St. Julian (The Order of Alcántara)
Founded: Around 1166, to protect the castle captured from the Moors, and other lands. Confirmed by the pope in 1177.

The Order of Knights of Calatrava
Founded: 1158, in Castile, Spain, to protect the plains of Calatrava, captured from the Moors in 1146, and Toledo and the routes to the south. Confirmed by the pope in 1164.

Merged with the Order of Monfragüe and the Order of Mountjoy in 1221.

The Knights of St. James of Compostela (The Order of Santiago)
Founded: 1170, in Léon. Confirmed by the pope in 1175.

The Order of Montegaudio
Founded: Late 1170s, and based mainly in Aragon. It later joined with the Knights Templar and the Hospital of the Holy Redeemer at Truel.

Order of the Blessed Virgin Mary of Mercy (and the Redemption of the Captives)
Founded: 1218, in Barcelona, for the ransoming of poor Christian slaves captured by Muslims.

POLAND

Order of Dobrzyń
Founded: Early thirteenth century, in Dobrzyń, by Christian of Oliva, first Bishop of Prussia, to protect against raids by pagan Prussian tribes. Confirmed by the pope in 1228. In 1235 most of the knights joined the Teutonic Knights.

PORTUGAL

The Knights of Aviz
Founded: 1128, as a separate order of the Knights of Calatrava.

Order of the Knights of Our Lord Jesus Christ
Founded: 1319 by King Denis of Portugal. This was a renaming of the Knights Templar in Portugal so that lands and castles could be kept, and the knights could continue to protect against the Moors and help rebuild the country.

The Teutonic Order gained many properties in eastern Europe such as Bytów Castle in Poland, built in 1398.

ENGLAND AGAINST FRANCE: THE HUNDRED YEARS' WAR

Actually lasting even more than a hundred years – from 1337 to 1453 – the Hundred Years' War developed from clashes between the English and French monarchies. Ever since the Norman Conquest of England in 1066 the English kings held huge estates in France and were thus vassals of the French monarchy, a position they resented and challenged at every opportunity. In addition, at various times the English rulers felt that they had a claim to the French throne itself, a claim they were willing to assert by force.

More properly a series of wars rather than one continuous conflict, the Hundred Years' War was a major event of the Middle Ages, bringing in various allies of the main combatants. It had several different stages, including long periods of peace. From 1337 to 1360 battles were fought to determine control of the Duchy of Guyenne, compounded by Edward III of England making a claim to the French throne. From 1360 till 1413 there was a period of stalemate, truces, and inconclusive warfare, followed by an active era that saw Henry V of England

Joan of Arc leading her forces to Orléans.

lead decisive victories before dying young. The saint Joan of Arc led a French resistance, and, intertwined with the main players, the dukes of the medieval state of Burgundy influenced the course of the war.

BACKGROUND TO WAR

In 1327 Edward III ascended to the English throne. The nephew of the French king Charles IV through his mother Isabella, he owned so much territory in France that he was the most important vassal of the French kings. The following year Charles IV died without leaving a son, so Edward believed he was the rightful heir. However, the French barons crowned Philip VI, a cousin of Charles, as king.

Having settled his English realm, Edward responded furiously when Philip attempted to confiscate the English-owned Aquitaine in 1337, and immediately declared war, announcing his claim to the French throne. The situation was aggravated by new taxes imposed by the French crown in order to raise money, which particularly affected towns in northern France that had become wealthy through the cloth trade. Relying on English wool for their raw material, many towns supported England in the conflict.

IMPACT OF WAR

Fought almost entirely in France, the Hundred Years' War saw several parts of northern France devastated, not just during times of conflict, but even during truces, since the war saw the introduction of mercenaries by both

Besieging a town. Early cannon were used during the war.

THE COURSE OF CONFLICT

1337 Battle of Cadsand
Hostilities began

1340 Battle of Sluys
At this sea battle England defeated the French-Genoese fleet off the coast of Flanders. The victory prevented an invasion of England, and ensured that the war would be fought in France.

1346 Battle of Crécy
The longbowmen of the English army helped destroy French cavalry. 1,542 French knights were killed, as well as thousands of infantry.

1346–7 Siege of Calais
After a siege of nearly a year, Calais fell to the English.

1356 Battle of Poitiers
The English heir, Edward the Black Prince, captured King John II of France.

1372 Battle of La Rochelle
A French-Castilian fleet broke English control of the seas, leading to a series of French raids on English ports.

1415 Battle of Agincourt
Once again the longbowmen of the English army proved decisive as Henry V inflicted a serious defeat upon the French.

1419 Siege of Rouen
After a six-month siege, England took the town and won a foothold in Normandy.

1428–9 Siege of Orléans
Joan of Arc forced English troops to withdraw.

1453 Battle of Castillon
A French victory that effectively ended the war. One of the first battles in Europe during which cannon played a major part in the victory.

The Battle of Agincourt.

sides. When not employed, these forces simply roamed the countryside, stealing what they wanted. The old feudal reliance upon vassals supplying knights and men-at-arms began to break down.

The era of the mounted knight came to an end during the conflict. Crossbows and the English or Welsh longbow were used to plow down knights, meaning that open warfare had to change. The war also saw some of the first engagements in Europe that used artillery. In addition, so many towns were besieged during the war that the technology of siege warfare developed rapidly during the hundred years of warfare.

Fighting cost money, and in order to pay for the war England and France introduced unpopular new taxes. This contributed to social unrest, and both countries experienced revolts: the Jacquerie peasant uprising of 1358 in France, and Wat Tyler's Peasants Revolt of 1381 in England. In addition, France supported Welsh rebels and Scottish raiders, ensuring that the English kings were kept busy at home.

THE OUTCOME

Although in the early fifteenth century it seemed that England might be going to carve out a new kingdom in part of France, in the end, after more than a hundred years of sporadic conflict, the English were left owning no French territory except for the town of Calais. Even Aquitaine, once a personal holding of the English royal family, had been acquired by France, although not without a revolt from the region. As England then became embroiled in civil war – the Wars of the Roses – English kings put aside their claim to the French throne, although it was centuries before they formally relinquished the claim. Another outcome of the war was the beginning of nationalism in both England and France.

MUSLIM SPAIN

For centuries Iberia was ruled over by foreigners, first by the Romans, then by the Germanic tribes who created Visigothic kingdoms. So when the Arabs and Berbers from North Africa arrived in 711 and defeated the Visigothic aristocracy, there was little resistance from ordinary people in the lands that are now Spain and Portugal.

As well as the aloof Basque country, European kingdoms survived in the mountainous northwest of Spain, but at first they had little help from from other Christian countries or from within al-Andalus, as the Arabs called their new country (meaning "land of the Vandals"). Instead, al-Andalus grew to become part of the Arab Golden Age, a prosperous, glorious civilization where arts and sciences flourished, Jews and Christians were not only tolerated but were given court positions, and where advanced agricultural techniques were introduced to the continent.

Under the Ummayad dynasty founded by Abd-al-Rahman I in 756, Cordoba in particular became a major cultural center and the biggest city in Europe. Clean and well-lit, the city housed about 79 libraries, as well as public baths

Jews in 14th-century Arab Spain found less discrimination there than they did in Christian lands.

and drinking fountains, running water, sewers, and public toilets. The Great Mosque was one of the wonders of the Muslim world. Toledo was another center of technology and literature, while the 14th-century Alhambra palace in Grenada (meaning "red fortress") was a stunning architectural achievement.

THE RECONQUISTA

Christian reconquest (the Reconquista) was begun by the nascent kingdom of the Asturias leading raids into al-Andalus. By 911 Asturia had doubled in size, moving the capital to the city of León. By then they had fortified the frontier, creating a new territory known as Castile (the land of castles), and it was the kingdom of Castile–León which, by 1085, extended its authority over much of southern Spain, including Toledo. Other small Christian states began to merge into stronger polities that were also able to encroach upon al-Andalus, but the full reconquest was to take centuries more.

After the collapse of the Cordoban caliphate in 1031, al-Andalus fragmented into about 30 small, local kingdoms, and these turned for help to a new North African dynasty, the militant Almoravids, who fought the Castilians to a standstill and then seized control of al-Andalus for themselves. Puritanical and fanatical, they persecuted or exiled Christians and Jews, forcing many of them to flee to the Christian kingdoms. However, in turn, the Almoravids were overcome by an even more puritanical North African dynasty, the Almohads.

EL CID

The great hero of the early Reconquista was the Castilian knight Rodrigo Díaz de Vivar (1043–99), popularly known as El Cid. His title derives from the Arabic *sidi* or *sayyid*, meaning "lord" or "master," and he is also known as the "Campeador" (Spanish for

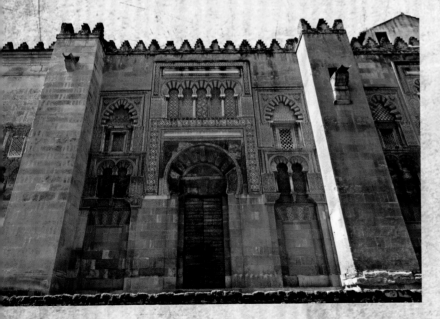

The Great Mosque at Cordoba.

various times he fought for Castile, León, Aragon, and Catalania against the Muslims, and created his own fiefdom around Valencia.

In the early stages of the Reconquista the Christian leaders simply wanted control of territory and peoples, and took tribute and allegiance from the conquered Muslims or Moors. However, from 1064 the popes supported formal religious crusades against the Muslims in the peninsula, and the great military orders of the Knights Templars and Hospitallers established powerful bases in Christian Spain. Other crusading orders were founded in the area, such as the Knights of Calatrava (1157), the Order of Alcántara (1165), and the Order of Santiago (1170). Even so, the Christian kingdoms did occasionally form alliances with Muslim kingdoms in power-struggles amongst themselves, but from then on, the Christian reconquest did not absorb or assimilate Muslims, instead it forced them away.

In 1212 Alfonso VIII of Castile, supported by the other major Christian kingdoms of Aragon, Navarre, and Portugal, won an important battle at Las Navas de Tolosa, and by the middle of the century the emirate of Granada in the southeast was the only remaining major Muslim state, and that survived only by paying annual tribute. However, the Reconquista did not formally end until the fifteenth century, when Granada was besieged and fell in 1492, a momentous year in Spanish history since it saw Ferdinand of Aragon and Isabella of Castile marry and begin the process of unifying Spain, Christopher Columbus make his world-changing journey to the New World, and the expulsion of Jews from Spain.

TURKISH ATTACKS

The other major Muslim encroachment upon Christian Europe was further east. The original expansion by the Arabs in the seventh century gave them control of Cyprus and Rhodes for a while, from where they continuously launched attacks on Constantinople. But it was much later, in the fourteenth century, that Byzantium was seriously threatened, by the Ottoman Turks. Originating in central Asia and gradually moving westwards, the Ottomans Turks expanded into Europe after the battle of Kosovo in Serbia in 1389 in which both forces were decimated but the Ottomans were enabled to proceed into the Balkans.

In 1371 the Ottomans took Thrace and Macedonia, then Bulgaria and Albania before the jewel, Constantinople itself, fell in 1453. Greece, Serbia, and Bosnia soon followed, and Turkish forces then threatened Italy and Austria. The sieges of Vienna took place after the Middle Ages – in 1529 and 1683 – but during the late Middle Ages Europeans were well aware that a fearsome enemy, the "Saracens," awaited at the gates.

MONGOL HORDES

The other great enemies who affected European history were the Mongols. Nomads from the plains of what is now Mongolia, they were united by Ghenghis Khan (1165–1227), who founded the largest undivided land empire in history, reaching at its height from the China Sea to central Europe. Often called Tartars, Mongols of the Golden Horde devastated Eastern Europe, creating a power vacuum that changed the face of the region.

The Mongols first tested Europe with an attack on Kievan Rus in 1223. They returned in 1237 as a full-scale invasion force, sacking Kiev in 1240, passing through Poland, burning Krakow in 1241, devasting Romania, killing Henry II of Silesia at Leignitz (Legnica), and destroying the Hungarian army at Mohi. Henry's army included Teutonic Knights and French Knights Templar, and after the decisive defeat, the Grand Master of the Knights Templar warned King Louis IX of France that there was now no significant European army standing between the Mongols and France.

However, western Europe was saved from invasion. Instead, the Mongols turned back and in 1242 withdrew from Europe as suddenly as they had appeared when they returned to Mongolia to elect a new Great Khan. From then on, although there were raids into eastern Europe, the Mongols' attention was focused on other parts of the world.

Despite their short time in Europe, the Mongols had a lasting impact. They showed that even the cream of European knights could be destroyed by disciplined, determined, and efficient soldiers, which most European armies of the time were not. Many historians believe that they introduced gunpowder, whose use they had learnt from China, into Europe. They also created power vacuums in their wake, enabling the Duchy of Moscow to gain influence in Russia.

RELIGION

EARLY MEDIEVAL CHRISTIANITY

Medieval life was completely dominated by Christianity. From birth to death, the stages of life were overseen by the Church, and the word of a priest, a bishop, or a pope was final in all areas to do with piety, morality, spirituality, and righteousness. The threat of punishment in Hell for sins, and the fear of excommunication, or being cut out of the Church and going straight to Hell after death, kept most people faithfully following the dictates of the Church.

CHURCH AND STATE

When Christianity was adopted as the state religion in the Western Roman Empire in 380, the emperor took control of the new religion, appointing the bishops, using them as local administrators, and approving the Church liturgy. With the fall of Rome, the Church became the *de facto* guardian of scholarship, law, and the civil and moral insitutions of the Empire, and represented stability in the midst of social chaos. Its very structure mirrored that of Rome: geographical districts called dioceses, each ruled over by a bishop who was based in a central urban area – his seat or see, with Rome, the "first among equals," the most significant see. The Church thus cemented its important role in society, and when the new kingdoms of western Europe converted, the Church was reluctant to give up any of its secular authority. At first, it was not asked to. The new kings found that Christianity gave them a link to the status of the Roman Empire, so they granted bishops a wide degree of authority. It was only later that clashes occurred between secular and religious powers.

Under Charlemagne, the Church gained even more power. He saw the role of king

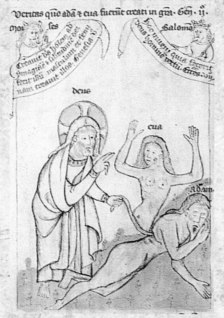

Above: The creation of Eve: medieval art was dominated by religious themes.
Below: Senior churchmen used beautiful and valuable treasures, including their personal crosses.

as a religious office, and felt that secular law was religious law. The new relationship between Church and State was cemented in 800 when Pope Leo III assumed he had the authority to crown Charlemagne as Emperor of the Franks, a new Roman Emperor, but this time a Holy one.

However, when Charlemagne's empire crumbled into much smaller realms, and the hierarchy of feudalism took hold in Europe, the secular power of the Church also crumbled. By 1000 the nobles took upon themselves the right to appoint bishops and priests within their areas of control, and the Church became decentralized, divided, and corrupt.

MONASTERIES

A feature of Early Medieval Christianity was the development of the ascetic monastic way of life, where devotees lived in self-sufficient communities under the rule of an abbot, and aspired to "pray and work." In western Europe a particularly influential event was the foundation of a monastery at Monte Casino in Italy in 529 by St. Benedict (480–543), and his "rule" or code became the lasting guide for monastic living.

The word monk comes from the Greek *monos*, meaning "alone," since the first monks were hermits in the wilderness. Even when they began to group together in monasteries, some of their members were recluses who did not share in community living, but instead lived in seclusion. Monastic life drew many women (nuns), and it was one of the few areas of life in which women could exercise authority.

In contrast to the settled monks, mendicant friars traveled around and depended upon charitable alms for their livelihood.

THE CELTIC CHURCH

For a time it seemed as if the Celtic Church

that developed in Britain, with its illuminated manuscripts, high crosses, intricate metalwork, a different date for Easter, and a tonsure for monks running from ear to ear instead of in the center of the head, would be a permanent challenge to the Roman Church. However, at the Synod of Whitby in 664 the British Christians mostly accepted the strictures of Rome.

They left to the world a legacy of one of the most magnificent illustrated gospels of the Middle Ages, the *Book of Kells*. Created about the year 800, it is an ornate, complex masterpiece of calligraphy, combining British themes such as animals, mythological creatures, and Celtic knots with standard Christian symbolism.

THE ICONOCLAST CONTROVERSY

In Eastern Europe the Early Middle Ages saw the Iconoclast Controversy that divided the Byzantine empire. In 730 Emperor Leo III adopted the religious stance which argued that icons and religious images of Christ were idolotrous, and should be removed from churches and state buildings. He was supported by the Byzantine army, so despite popular opposition his view prevailed, and countless icons, statues, and paintings were destroyed. Only in 843 were icons permitted again, by Theodora, widow of Emperor Theophilus.

LATER MEDIEVAL CHRISTIANITY

In the later medieval centuries the Christian Church was characterized by division and corruption as well as by glorious art and great-souled people who were canonized as saints.

THE GREAT SCHISM

For most of the Middle Ages, only the Roman, Latin, or Catholic Church (meaning "universal") was accepted in western Europe, while in eastern Europe the Eastern (or Greek) Orthodox Church was dominant. The two churches disagreed about the authority of Rome and Byzantium, about details of the Eucharist or Holy Communion, and spent much energy excommunicating each other's representatives. Eventually, they separated formally in 1054 in what is called the Great Schism. Despite centuries of negotiation, the schism was confirmed at the Synod of Constantinople in 1484.

Non-Orthodox groups were dealt with firmly by the Catholic Church, for example Crusades or Holy Wars were declared against the Waldensian, Albigensian, and Cathar sects in southern France, who denounced the authority of popes and claimed to receive individual enlightenment. Anyone thought to be a heretic was executed (often in horrible ways), and the Inquisition, first established in 1184, used torture to convince suspects to confess and repent.

CORRUPTION

The horrors of the Inquisition were only one aspect of late medieval Church corruption. In his *Canterbury Tales*, written between 1387 and 1400, Geoffrey Chaucer highlighted the behavior of summoners and pardoners, ecclesiastical officials

who took bribes or offered indulgences (remitting punishment for sins) for money. In addition, hawkers sold so-called "relics" such as pieces of the True Cross or bones of saints, while many medieval popes were known to be controlled by powerful secular rulers.

CHURCH AND STATE RESOLVED

The ongoing tension between secular rulers and popes reached a compromise in 1122 with the Concordat of Worms. In this settlement, religious officials accepted that their temporal overlord had the power to invest them with secular authority. But in the early fourteenth century the French state began to control the papacy.

THE AVIGNON PAPACY

From 1309 to 1376 the popes held court in Avignon in France, rather than in Rome. This change followed the election of Clement V, a Frenchman, who refused to move to Rome, and who was followed by six other French popes. The period is sometimes referred to as the "Babylonian Captivity of the Papacy."

THE GREAT WESTERN SCHISM

Throughout the Middle Ages there were so-called "antipopes," rival popes who disputed the authority of the pope acknowledged

Church reformer John Wycliffe; Pope Gregory IX, whose papacy ran from 1227 to 1241, clashed with the Holy Roman Emperor Frederick Barbarossa over Church rights.

by the majority. In 1378 the power struggle for the papacy came to a head when two men were elected in the same year. The cardinals soon regretted their first candidate, Urban VI, who quickly became a violent, suspicious, and dominating ruler, so later that year they met again and elected Clement VII, who set up court in Avignon, France. For decades thereafter there were two popes, compounded by yet a third antipope in 1409 when Alexander V was elected by a new convocation. Only in 1414 did the Council of Constance organize the resignation of rival claimants and elected in their place Pope Martin V in 1417.

CONTROL OF KNOWLEDGE

For most of the Middle Ages the Bible was only known in Latin, which was the language of scholarship, religion, and knowledge. Schools were attached to cathedrals, or individual clerics taught the sons of noblemen, so the Church controlled all learning. One of the first people to oppose this grip on knowledge was the Englishman John Wycliffe (c.1328–84) who in 1382 translated the Bible into English and supported the view that Christians should emulate Christ by living in poverty. His followers, known as Lollards, continued his work, but in 1415 he was declared a heretic and his body was later dug up and burnt.

PILGRIMAGES

By going on a pilgrimage to holy sites or shrines, ordinary people hoped that God would forgive them their sins and that they would be allowed into heaven, or that illnesses would be miraculously cured. The Church promoted this ideal, encouraging pilgrims to visit shrines where relics of saints or of the Holy Cross were kept. At each site, pilgrims would have to pay to see the relic, and along pilgrimage routes the abbeys and monasteries where pilgrims would stay for the night grew wealthy.

Jerusalem, Rome, and Santiago de Compostela were the three most holy pilgrimage sites, necessitating long, dangerous journeys. In Britain Canterbury Cathedral, the place where St. Thomas à Becket was killed, was a popular destination, as shown in Chaucer's *Canterbury Tales*. Pilgrims banded together for safety, and the military monastic order, the Knights Templar, was set up specifically to protect the pilgrimage routes to Jerusalem.

Having paid their money to pray at the shrines, pilgrims

Santiago de Compostela in Spain, one of the great pilgrim destinations.

were given a metal badge to show that they had visited the holy site, with the scallop shell of St. James, indicating Santiago de Compostela, a famous symbol.

Left: The Council of Constance 1414–18 which settled the three-popes controversy and elected Pope Martin V.
Right: Jesus shown in contemporary dress after his resurrection.
Below: The magnificent illuminated decoration in the Book of Kells.

THE MAJOR MONASTIC ORDERS OF THE MIDDLE AGES

Augustinians, founded in 1256, named after St. Augustine.

Benedictines, founded in 529 by St. Benedict, emphasis on manual labor in a self-sufficient monastery.

Carmelites, founded in the late twelfth century as an order of contemplative prayer.

Carthusians or Cistercians, founded by St. Bernard of Clairvaux in 1098. Acknowledging the Virgin Mary as a saint, this was the first Christian group to give a woman an important position within the religion.

Celestines, a branch of the Carmelites, founded in 1244.

Cluniacs, 878 onwards, a reforming movement aiming to cut out corruption.

Dominicans, approved by the Vatican in 1216, its members aimed to wipe out heresy.

Franciscans, founded by St. Francis of Assisi around 1209. The Order of St. Clare or Poor Clares were the second, women's order.

CIVILIZATION AMONGST THE HORRORS: MEDIEVAL SAINTS

Amidst all the horrors of medieval Europe, some individuals stood out as examples of good, holiness, and piety. After their deaths they were canonized, or officially recognized as saints by the Catholic Church. Their ranks include:

Bernard of Clairvaux
Francis of Assisi
Hildegard of Bingen
Joan of Arc
Louis IX of France
Thomas à Becket of Canterbury

The theological philosophers Thomas Aquinas and Albertus Magnus were also canonized, as were Clare, who created the Poor Clare monastic order for women, and Ludmilla, who is credited with developing Christianity in Bohemia.

Saints were people who were thought to be so filled with Christ's spirit that they became worthy of veneration. Some worked miracles, others brought new religious teachings to the world, and some believed so strongly in Christianity that they suffered and died for their faith. To the common people of the Middle Ages saints were particularly significant, since they were originally ordinary people themselves, and thus not only promised the hope of saintliness to everyone, but were also more approachable than God. They were individuals who could intercede between humanity and deity, and could carry prayers to heaven.

There were two main categories of Roman Catholic saints: martyrs and confessors. Martyrs were killed, while confessors died natural deaths. The bodies of all saints were considered to be holy, so parts of their remains were treasured as holy relics, kept in special containers called reliquaries, and sometimes only brought out into public view for special occasions such as the saint's feast day. Saints became patrons of countries, such as St. George of England, or of professions and ideas, such as

Above: St. Louis.
Left: The lives of the saints gave religious and spiritual inspiration to ordinary people. But at a time when there were few secular diversions, stories of the saints were also a source of entertainment. Here St. Wolfgang defeats a demon.
Right: The more devout you were, the more chance that a saint would intervene for you. In this early 14th century painting, St. Humility is healing a sick nun.

St. Christopher, patron saint of travelers, and some became so popular that cults grew up around their veneration.

Pre-Christian deities such as Bride or Bridgit of Ireland were adopted into the Christian religion as saints so that ordinary people felt a continuity of local spirituality, and medieval festivals were nearly always held under the aegis of a saint's day.

ST. FRANCIS OF ASSISI

Born Giovanni Francesco di Bernardone in 1181 or 1182, St. Francis was the son of a wealthy Italian cloth merchant, and spent the first part of his life in the secular world. In 1204, while fighting as a soldier, he had a religious vision that eventually sent him on pilgrimage to Rome, where he met the beggars around the Vatican. This influenced him to begin a life of poverty, and he became a poor preacher, delivering his message on the streets of his native Assisi.

Above left: An Eastern Church manuscript depicting St. Basil.
Above right: In Bede's *Life of St. Cuthbert*, news of the saint's death is signaled to his brethren.
Right: St. Jerome studying in the wilderness, ignoring all temptations and irritations.

His themes of repentance and repudiation of worldly goods soon won him followers, and in 1210 the pope formally recognized his group as a religious order, the Franciscans. He and his followers were friars, who, unlike monks, were not attached to a building, and continued to preach on the streets and to forego all possessions. St. Francis also spent a great deal of time alone in retreat in the countryside.

In 1211 he helped the noblewoman Clare of Assisi to found the enclosed religious order for women that became known as the Poor Clares, and he also founded the Third Order of Brothers and Sisters of Penance for lay people (those who did not take religious orders) who could not leave their worldly lives.

In 1219 Francis traveled to Egypt, where he preached unsuccessfully to the sultan, then, back in Italy, in about 1220 he created the first-known three-dimensional nativity scene at Christmas so

Above left: Giotto's depiction of St. Francis casting devils out of the town of Arezzo, Tuscany. The church there is dedicated to him.
Above right: Angels prepare to carry St. Louis IX to heaven.
Right: A painting by Hildegard of Bingen.

that worshippers could more fully experience Christ's birth: he conducted Christmas mass in front of a manger set between a live ox and a live donkey.

In 1224 St. Francis was the first person known to display the stigmata, when bloody wounds appeared on his body similar to those experienced by Christ on the cross. He died in 1226 whilst preaching. As well as being the patron saint of animals, he is one of the patron saints of Italy, along with Catherine of Siena.

HILDEGARD OF BINGEN
As well as being a Christian mystic and abbess, St. Hildegard was a philosopher, a musician, a botanist, and an all-round polymath.

Born in the Palatine of the Rhine in the Holy Roman Empire (now Germany) around 1098, she was given to the church by her noble family when she was a child, and lived in an enclosed Benedictine community. In 1136 her fellow nuns elected her the abbess of the order, and the group became so successful that in 1165 Hildegard founded a second convent.

Throughout her life Hildegard experienced spiritual visions, which she began to record and interpret in Biblical terms from 1141 onwards. Overall, she left 100 letters, 72 songs, 70 poems, and 9 books. Around 1151 she wrote possibly the first morality play, *Ordo Virtutum* (*Play of the Virtues*), and her books were widely read, partly because Pope Eugenius III gave them his formal approval. Her musical compositions show a deep veneration of the Virgin Mary and of saints, while she also wrote on the natural sciences and on the healing properties of plants, minerals, and precious stones. Hildegard's spiritual and philosophical works also covered human sexuality.

During her lifetime women were not expected to have any authority either secular or spiritual, yet Hildegard was so influential that she was invited to preach in public. She often pointed out that she was uneducated, but this simply confirmed that her inspiration was divine. When she died in 1179 her religious sisters reported seeing two beams of light crossing over her room.

Above left: The martyrdom of Saints Peter and Paul.
Above right: St. Bernard. He was responsible for promoting the cult of Mary.
Right: St. Thomas à Becket.

CATHEDRALS

In an age without science to guide men and women, the world was a dangerous and uncertain place. Behind every unforeseen event – a plague, a war, the inexplicable death of a healthy man, a bad harvest – was discerned the invisible guiding hand of God. By his will everything came to pass. Prayer and devotion were believed to bring God's love and care, consequently religion was at the heart of medieval man and woman. Nothing reflected this more than the medieval mania for building cathedrals.

Technically a cathedral is defined as a church which contains the seat of a bishop. The first cathedrals were built by the Romans and were modelled on the square-shaped basilica, a type of public building found in most European cities in that time. During the Middle Ages the design of cathedrals changed dramatically, for in a world where most buildings were made of wood and rarely stood higher than two stories, medieval cathedrals were constructed from stone and soared hundreds of feet into the sky: they were the skyscrapers of the age.

No country built more cathedrals than France where, from 1050 to 1350, 80 cathedrals and 500 hundred large churches were constructed. More stone was excavated than in the entire history of ancient Egypt. But cathedrals were intended to be far more than a place of worship, they were meant to be nothing less than a physical mirror of heaven on earth, a meeting place between man and God.

Below left: St. Denis Cathedral, Paris, the first Gothic cathedral. Below right: The awe-inspiring front of Barcelona Cathedral, Spain. Facing page (top left) The steep points of Strasbourg Cathedral, France. Some of the earliest known architectural drawings were used to plan its west facade; (top right) Cologne Cathedral, the largest Gothic church in northern Europe; (below left) typical Gothic architecture at Reims, with bell towers and portals. Since 496 with the accession of Clovis, French kings were consecrated here. (below right) the Cathedral of Our Lady in Tournai, France, is a mixture of Gothic and Romanesque styles.

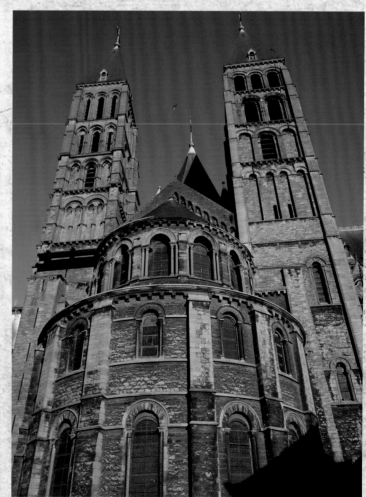

ST. DENIS

Although Byzantine styles influenced many early cathedrals in southern Europe, the Romanesque style – derived from classic Roman traditions – dominated in western Europe in the eleventh and twelfth centuries when monumental works were built again after the "Dark Ages." However, in 1135 an architectural revolution took place with the cathedral of St. Denis, Île-de-France. Work began in 1135 and when completed 20 years later, it was the tallest building in Europe. The designers incorporated several new architectural innovations such as pointed arches (which may have originated from the Muslim world) ribbed vaulting, and flying buttresses. These enabled St. Denis's walls to be tall yet thin, and filled with windows. Heaven was believed to be a bright and dazzling place, and in reflection of this the presence of so many windows illuminated St Denis unlike any previous building. The addition of stained glass brought colored light into the cathedral. The effect was unique, and one contemporary wrote that he felt himself transported "to some strange region of the universe between the slime of earth and the purity of heaven." This new, revolutionary style of architecture was known as Gothic, and would become the dominant style throughout the Middle Ages.

Above: (top left and right) Regional artistic styles were applied to church buildings, as in the unusual tiled roof of St. Stephen's Cathedral in Vienna, Austria, and the distinctive Romanesque design of of Speyer Cathedral, Germany. (bottom left) Detail of the intricate roof of the cathedral of St. Jan in s-Hertogenbosch, The Netherlands. (bottom right) St. Michael's Golden-Domed Cathedral, Kiev, Ukraine. Destroyed in the Soviet era, this is a reconstruction of the original medieval building.

CHARTRES

Some 60 years after St. Denis was begun, in 1193 the French town of Chartres, about 50 miles from Paris, built its own cathedral. Chartres was small, probably no bigger than 10,000 souls, yet the entire population helped quarry the stone needed for the cathedral's construction. After that, 300 craftsmen labored for a quarter of a century until the cathedral was finally completed. Since that time, the cathedral has hardly been altered; even the stained glass remains intact. It is regarded as the perfect example of a medieval cathedral and is a UNESCO world heritage site.

Chartres was built in the shape of a cross, the symbol of the Christian faith, and is orientated east-west, expressing man's advancement towards God. The main entrance is on the west, and is known as the Porte Royale.

It contains three portals all in all: the side portals are decorated with carvings of Old Testament kings and queens, the center portal is surmounted by a frieze of the day the Last Judgement, with Christ in the tympanum.

The interior of the cathedral is vast – the nave is 427 feet long (128 meters) and 121 feet wide (36 meters). In the center of the floor is a maze or labyrinth. At one time, every cathedral in Europe contained a similar maze, but Chartres' is one of the few to survive.

THE MAZE

Worshippers would have followed the maze on bended knees and in deep prayer along its constant, winding turns until they reached the center. It is thought that the maze symbolized the Holy City, and thus, to walk its path was a symbolic pilgrimage to Jerusalem.

Chartres Cathedral contains three large rose windows, round windows divided by spokes radiating from a central opening, and filled with stained glass. Rose windows are a distinctive feature of Gothic architecture.

By the thirteenth century no European city considered itself complete without a Gothic cathedral of its own. Since cathedrals were always built in the center of town, they were literally at the heart of the community, not only religiously but socially and economically, and markets were held not only on the cathedral steps, but inside as well. Textiles might be sold in the north transcept, meat and vegetables under the south porch. Money changers worked in the west portals, wine sellers stored wine in the crypt. In our own, modern, secular age, there are no comparable buildings which serve the community so fully. The Gothic cathedral was a unique institution which died with the Middle Ages.

Below: (top left) Inside Chartres Cathedral: a monument to God. (top right) The facade of Reims Cathedral, France. (bottom left) The labyrinth floor of Chartres Cathedral. (bottom right) The medieval masons paid attention to every inch of stone, as shown by these statues adorning Chartres Cathedral.

In general, medieval women were completely dominated by their menfolk: if unmarried they were considered to be the property of their fathers and brothers, and if they were married they became the property of their husbands.

This view of women's status came directly from the Church. Thomas Aquinas, the thirteenth-century Dominican priest and foremost theologian of the day said, "The woman is subject to man on account of the weakness of her nature. Man is the beginning of woman and her end, just as God is the beginning and end of every creature. Children should love their father more than their mother." He also said, "As regards the individual nature, woman is defective and misbegotten." Women were expected to be meek and submissive, could be beaten for disobedience, and hardly ever received a full education.

Even great queens such as Eleanor of Aquitaine (1122/24–1204) suffered because of their gender. She spent several years in prison, while Isabella (1295–1358), wife of Edward II of England, was derogatively called "the She-Wolf of France."

EXCEPTIONS

Some noble girls had private tutors, especially since they needed a degree of literacy to run the estates when their husbands were away at war. But oddly, it was the Church that offered most status for unmarried women. With the establishment of

An unusual woodcut from late medieval Germany entitled "Mistress Minne's Power over the Hearts of Men." It shows men's hearts being put through various forms of torture, while the lady looks on complacently.

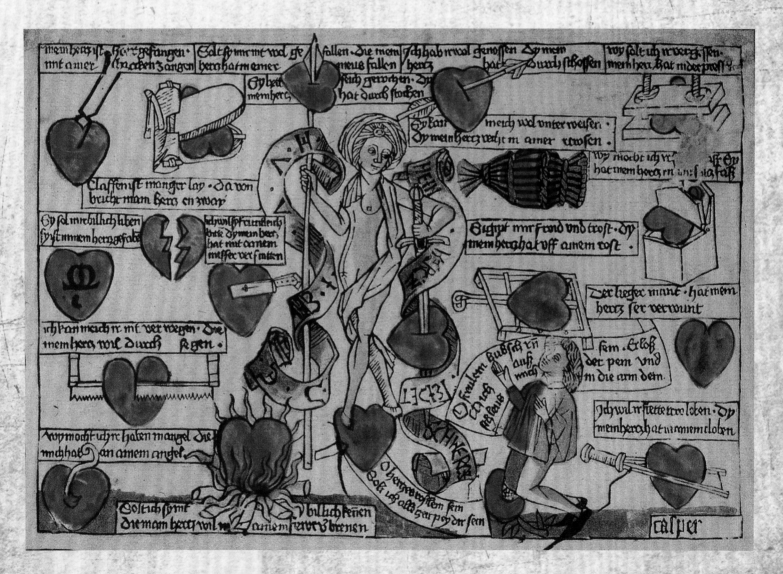

monasticism, women could become nuns and abbesses, holding power, land, and responsibilities, and sometimes they even ruled over monasteries of both monks and nuns. In addition, many women became mystical saints, such as Hildegard of Bingen and Julian of Norwich. But although women could receive an education in devout communities, they could not become bishops or deacons.

SOCIAL STANDING

Noble women often lived to the age of 70, although 90 percent of the population were peasants, and peasant women could be dead by 25. Life was harsh and there was little chance to escape it. Work in the fields lasted from dawn till dusk, and it was also women's responsibility to gather and peel rushes for lights, make and mend clothes, tend the food plots, and cook. A peasant woman was seen as worthless. She could not marry without the consent of the local lord, and her children

The perfect woman was, of course, the Virgin Mary.

could be referred to as "her litter." Grinding poverty, the perils of childbirth, hard toil to pay the rent and taxes to the lords, poor nutrition, and terrible living conditions were the lot of the medieval peasant woman.

Wealthier women had little say in who they would marry, and tended to marry earlier than peasant women. Often, the marriage was arranged by their fathers to suit dynastic aims or to cement alliances. The need to produce an heir for their husband was crucial and all women, regardless of status, were at risk of dying in childbirth. Noble women did not usually breastfeed, using poorer women as wet-nurses.

WORKING WOMEN

Apart from nobles, women were expected to work. Many single women earned a living from spinning, and the term "spinster"

for an unmarried woman comes from this activity. Unmarried women who owned property had the power to make a will and sign official documents, but once married, her property and land became her husband's. She would be entitled to one third of this on his death. When a peasant woman was widowed, the lord of the manor took a large part of the possessions. This was called taking *heriot*. Heriot included metal items, uncut cloth, all the pigs, sometimes the best of the other animals, and a fine. The church then claimed the second best beast, leaving widows and children in dire poverty. In addition, these unfortunate, unprotected widows were often accused of witchcraft.

Wives were expected to play an active role in their husband's businesses, and many of these women would be literate to some degree. Women could be artisans and have independent businesses, particularly brewing, but they needed permission to do so, and were paid less than men. There were female guilds until the sixteenth

Above left: Noble women had the leisure time and the education to play games such as chess.

Above right: Eleanor of Aquitaine inherited the Duchy of Aquitaine (Guyenne) and the County of Poitiers at the age of 15. Since they were then not part of France, she immediately became a wealthy and powerful woman. She added to her influence by marrying Louis VII of France and going on the Second Crusade with him, wearing mail. However she sought an annulment from their marriage and later married Henry Plantagenet, heir to the English throne and Duke of Normandy. He was to become Henry II of England, and their union created the massive Angevin empire.

When they became estranged and Eleanor helped her son Henry "the Young King" revolt against Henry II, she was imprisoned for 16 years, and was only freed when her son Richard the Lionheart became king. Well-educated and a great patron of the arts, she presided over the courtly love movement in Poitiers, and played a role in the governments of both England and Aquitaine, acting as regent for Richard when he was on crusade.

Left: Most women learnt how to spin.

Facing page: Serving God was considered to be a very suitable occupation for a woman.

century, when they became male-dominated and banned women, and by the end of the Middle Ages the role of women in society and business became increasingly restricted, as did women's rights to own property.

Weaving, household management, producing food, keeping the poultry and the dairy, caring for the sick when there was no local doctor were all tasks carried out by women. Noble women were expected to run the estate when their husbands were away, but they at least also had leisure for pastimes such as embroidery, weaving, and sometimes archery, while falconry and hunting were allowed for some ladies according to their rank.

TROUBADOURS AND THE CULT OF COURTLY LOVE

The medieval cult of Courtly Love began at the end of the eleventh century, at the time of the First Crusade.

It developed in the ducal and princely courts of Aquitaine, Burgundy, Champagne, and Provence of France, where marriage among nobility was concerned more with political allegiance than love and sexual attraction. The concept of Courtly Love offered an escape from these loveless arrangements, and was directed by a nobleman towards the real object of his heart's desire, who would be idealized and idolized, often to the status of a goddess. It was described as love from afar, "a love at once illicit and morally elevating, passionate and disciplined, humiliating and exalting, human and transcendent."

Courtly Love was carried out with an almost religious

devotion, playing upon the tension of an erotic attraction for an unattainable woman. The purpose was to transmute unfulfilled physical desire into a lofty spiritual state. This sublimated frustration and was satisfying because of the spiritual elevation. The lady held all the cards and the admirer yearned for the slightest hint of attention from her.

RULES

Courtly Love was governed by strict rules and etiquette. The protagonist would strive to make himself worthy of his lady. He had to be honorable and show courage at all times, and pass through ordeals and tests to win the lady's approval and honor, which she might or might not donate to him. She might bestow the prize of an occasional conversation with her admirer at court, or a comely glance or smile. She could also withhold favors, causing yearning, heartache, and jealousy, which was more grist to the mill of spiritual perfection. Being rejected was part of the game of Courtly Love.

The idolized lady would usually be of a higher rank at court than her admirer: the wife of the lord, duke, or even king, whose husband would often be away at war, on Crusade, or on business.

The unrequited love and the quest for the lady's respect were channeled into a knight's performance on the battlefield and in sports such as jousting, archery contests, and other tournaments. The protagonist was driven to excel to please his lady. As her champion, he would wear his lady's colors. She in turn might give the paladin a handkerchief or a glove, which would be a rare and highly erotically charged exchange. Such tokens were prized, and if personal items such as a lock of hair or fragment of clothing were obtained or bestowed, these could be pinned to the shield in battle or worn next to the heart.

Above: A minstrel as depicted on a stained glass window.
Left: Adenet le Roi, called King of the Minstrels, recites to Blanche of Castile (1188–1252) wife of Louis VIII of France, and Mathilde de Brabant, Countess of Artois.
Facing page: The Queen of the Tournament delivers the prizes.

The romantic lovers would have secret trysts and communicate with signs in a highly stylized code, imagining that these were not detected by other member of the court. The eyes played a significant role between the romantic lovers, with looks and glances giving great meaning. The lover could also declare his undying love and his exaltation of the lady with poetry.

The cult of Courtly Love drew on classical texts and also Arabic practices of morality and eroticism, which knights would have encountered on Crusade in the East and from Muslim Spain. Some scholars think the practice may have evolved in Muslim lands, although other influences came from the persecuted Cathar religious sect of the Languedoc and their teachings about purity and the rejection of the flesh.

TROUBADOURS

Courtly Love was particularly expressed in the lyrics of the troubadours, who spoke about the idealized soul of the "Lady." Comprising educated minstrels, poets, and actors, the troubadour movement began in Occitania, (now part of southern France), in the eleventh century and spread across Europe. They traveled extensively, but performed in one place under the patronage of a wealthy man or lady. The early troubadours were from the nobility, but later they came from all backgrounds. The thirteenth century saw the introduction of female troubadours, known as *troubairitz*, the first female composers of secular music. Many of the patrons of the troubadours were Cathars, and so the singers were influenced by the Cathar teachings. But the church overshadowed all aspects of life, and disapproved of the sensual lyrics, the role of women, and the connection with Cathars, even though the concept of Courtly Love elevated sexual desire to a noble ideal and contained a strong moral code.

By the thirteenth century the Church came to see Courtly Love as heretical. Coupled with the devastation caused by the Black Death, the cult all but disappeared. Traces of it survive in the Arthurian Legends, where the code is broken by Lancelot and Guinevere, and in fairytales of princes or knights and their arduous quests and tribulations to get to the Lady, such as Sleeping Beauty. Courtly Love and the troubadours are also present in the work of Chaucer, Chretien de Troyes, and Thomas Malory.

Eleanor of Aquitaine, Queen to Henry II, brought Courtly Love to England, and it was practiced in the English courts from the 1300s to the 1500s

The term "Courtly Love" to explain this phenomenon is nineteenth-century in origin, and it has been suggested that the practice of it outside of literature is nothing but a Victorian romantic invention. Scholars are divided on this, but generally come down in favor of an genuine cult of Courtly Love.

Facing page and below: Images from the Manesse Codex, a book of German love poetry depicting different poets or minnesingers celebrating love. The facing page shows the poet Johannes Hadlaub who probably helped compile the book. The bottom picture shows Dietmar von Aist disguised as a pedlar to woo his lady.

THE ARTS

Medieval European arts covered such a vast time scale and geographical area that it is difficult to categorize them. There were many local styles during the period, but in general art historians tend to describe medieval art under seven headings:

- Early Christian / Late Antique
- Migration period
- Byzantine
- Insular
- Pre-Romanesque
- Romanesque
- Gothic

During the so-called Dark Ages at the beginning of the medieval period most artistic works were rare and valuable, and only the ruling elite or religious institutions owned them. Such treasures were coveted by raiders, and monasteries and churches were often attacked for their gold and silver plate and other artefacts. However, by the end of the period many hard-working burghers and merchants in towns and rural farmers would also be able to own and enjoy beautiful pieces of art.

The European Middle Ages inherited a wide range of artistic styles from the eastern and western

Illustrated manuscripts required several artistic abilities: lettering, drawing, writing or poetry.

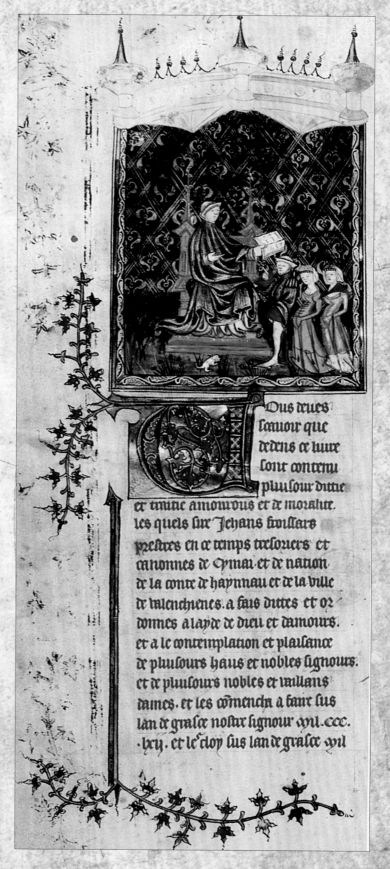

108

Roman Empires, from early Christianity, and from the various "barbarian" peoples who migrated to Europe. This fusion created a vibrant artistic legacy expressed in just about every medium: glassware, metalwork, jewelry, stained glass, wood, stone and ivory carving, mosaics, tapestries, painting, illuminated manuscripts, and monumental architecture.

Medieval artists loved to use expensive materials such as gold leaf and the rare deep blue color obtained from ground lapiz lazuli that was a feature of many depictions of the Virgin Mary's robes. Valuable materials such as vellum (calves' skins and paper) were saved, scraped clean, and re-used, which means that we have an ongoing record of medieval art.

EARLY CHRISTIAN / LATE ANTIQUE

Found mainly in the churches, catacombs, coins, sarcophagi, and mosaics of the late Roman world, art became less representational and more mystical. Another change was that portraits were no longer painted in profile, but in full face, staring at the viewer.

MIGRATION PERIOD

During the centuries that Germanic people were migrating around Europe most artistic effort was put into decorating practical objects that could be easily carried around: jewelry, tools, weapons. Many people were buried with their wealth, leaving a lasting record of the artistic styles of the times: a polychrome style in the Black Sea area; an animal style in northern Europe; and Celtic, Mediterranean, or other localized motifs.

During this period the Church became a major patron of the arts, commissioning beautiful equipment and sponsoring illuminated manuscripts that became a feature of Anglo-Saxon Christian art.

Left: A fifteenth-century tapestry depicting the Adoration of the Magi. Woven tapestries were not only objets d'art (usually depicting religious scenes), but they also had a practical use as wall hangings, door screens, and bed surrounds. Nobles would carry them from one estate to another as they traveled around. A time-consuming craft, the great weaving centers were Flanders and France, and by the mid-15th century there were about 15,000 workers in the industry in the Loire Valley alone.
Right: The Virgin Mary was often depicted wearing dark blue, as in this altarpiece painting by Flemish artist Hugo van der Goes.
Below: Typical Byzantine art from the dome of the Church of the Holy Savior, Chora, Istanbul (formerly Byzantium/Constantinople). The building is now a museum.

BYZANTINE STYLE

For about 1000 years the icons and architecture of Byzantium were a feature of east European art, and continue to influence Eastern Orthodox countries even today. Byzantine art differed from the Classical Greek representative style by becoming abstract, symbolic, and "anti-naturalistic," concentrating almost exclusively upon religious or imperial themes.

Icons, mosaics and ceramics, metalwork, carved ivory, illuminated manuscripts, and metalwork are all features of Byzantine art, and unlike western Europe, in religious buildings the Byzantines did not create monumental sculptures, but instead worked with reliefs.

INSULAR ART

A continuation of the Migration Period art in the British Isles, this style of Hiberno-Saxon art combined Celtic styles such as intricate knotwork with Anglo-Saxon techniques of animalistic representations. It flourished in British monasteries and in items for the ruling elite, and was interrupted by the Viking raids in the ninth century before merging with later artistic movements. Illuminated manuscripts, carved stone crosses, and intricate jewelry are all features of this style.

PRE-ROMANESQUE

From about 500 to 1000 in continental western Europe the new Germanic kingdoms absorbed classical artistic styles

Above: Although Christianity was the main subject of art, medieval craftsmen showed their sense of humor in many whimsical items, such as this odd monster on Windsor Castle Church in England and the gargoyles of Notre Dame cathedral overlooking overlooking Paris.
Left: Romanesque angels from an eleventh-century illuminated manuscript.

which merged with their native art forms to produce a new, original style. There were separate periods such as the Carolingian Renaissance and the Ottonian period (named after the three Ottos who ruled the Holy Roman Empire in the 900s), but in general this era reflected the late classical period, as both temporal rulers and church leaders were keen to assert their links to past traditions. Illuminated manuscripts are a particular feature of the period.

ROMANESQUE

Romanesque architecture contained many details of late Roman buildings, such as rounded arches, apses, and barrel vaulting. However, in painting, sculptures, and other

decorative arts it was a new and unique style, influenced by Byzantine art from the east and Anglo-Saxon art from the northwest. Romanesque art is the first style that was adopted throughout Europe.

Left: Painting of the Madonna and Child by the important Italian artist Cimabue (1240–1302). Below: (clockwise from top left) The Gothic sculptures in Strasbourg Cathedral. Intricate detail was given to all artistic works, such as this detail around the great clock in Prague. Early medieval brooches: jewelry was an easy way to carry wealth around. The twelfth-century Eltenberg Reliquary. Created to hold holy relics, reliquaries were often made out of precious materials; this one contains copper-gilt, ivory, and enamel.

This period saw the widespread use of stained glass, with church windows, the capitals of columns, and illuminated manuscripts all depicting a much wider range of subjects than in previous times, when the only scenes created were imperial themes and the major biblical stories. Churches were adorned with more carvings than before, although some elements of the past continued, since landscapes were nothing but abstract backgrounds and the size of figures represented their importance. Free-standing statues of the Virgin Mary were popular, but in a stylized, Byzantine form. There were practically no individual portraits created. Tapestry-making began to flourish.

GOTHIC

In about 1150 this style developed in France from the preceeding Romanesque art forms. Best known for its architecture that can be seen in the soaring cathedrals and grim fortresses of the time, Gothic art also took the form of monumental sculpture, frescoes, illuminated manuscripts, and panel paintings. It was popular all over Europe, especially in Germany where the style continued well into the sixteenth century, long after more naturalistic Renaissance artistic styles had been adopted elsewhere.

Carvings in churches became more allegorical, depicting scenes from the Old and New Testaments side by side, and figures were portrayed in a less stylized form.

LATE MIDDLE AGES

For the first time in Europe secular art became important as an educated, wealthy middle class began to commission artistic pieces of all sorts, from portraits to candlesticks and dinner plates. Painting in oils was introduced in the late fourteenth century, and as literature became written in vernacular languages and on secular subjects, the topics of illustrations widened from purely religious themes. Another innovation of the time was that artists joined trade guilds and began to sign their pieces, leaving a record of their individual work.

MUSIC

With the Church dominating so much of life, early medieval music that has survived until today was mainly religious. During the first centuries of the Middle Ages special church choirs developed to perform the musical roles in church services, and in the late sixth century women were banned from choirs, a tradition that lasted for centuries.

A major musical event was the codification of church music by Gregory I, pope from 590 until 604. The vocal chants (plainsong or plainchant) that he collected are still usually called Gregorian chants.

Secular music is more widely known from the eleventh century onwards as the political grip of the Church weakened and kings or nobles began to patronize musicians. Instrumental music began to develop in line with new vocal styles, performed by traveling minstrels or jongleurs who entertained with popular songs, by troubadours or trouvères who sang of courtly love, and by minnesingers who wrote love songs imbued with religious meaning.

Musical instruments included drums, harps, flutes, bagpipes, trumpets, and organs, as well as instruments that are less popular nowadays such as the lute (a wooden, plucked string instrument with a neck) and the psaltery (a small, portable, harp-like, stringed instrument).

This page: Typical medieval musical instruments: a bowed psaltery, recorders, a curved pan-flute, and a lute.
Facing page: Gothic architecture developed in the great cathedrals of Europe, but was later used for secular buildings such as Old City Hall, Gouda, Netherlands, built between 1448 and 1450.

FOOD IN THE MIDDLE AGES

While the majority of people in the Middle Ages faced a dull daily fare, for the lucky few many mealtimes were an opportunity for drama and spectacle. A noble's feast was more than just a meal: it was a magical entertainment.

A medieval lord would expect his head cook to be an artist, not just combining ingredients in an artistic manner, but also presenting the food in a way that would draw applause and admiration.

RANGE OF FOODS

For the better off, there was a huge range of foodstuffs available. Meats included beef, mutton, and pork, and since few parts were wasted, offal dishes were common. All types of birds were eaten, from swans and herons to pigeons and larks, as well as the geese and chickens that would be kept on the estate. Fish and shellfish included eels and lampreys, and many noble houses or monasteries would have fish-ponds to ensure a regular supply.

Dairy produce, fruits, many vegetables, and milled wheat were also regularly available to the wealthier sections of society, along with wines and spirits. Raw vegetables were considered to be bad for the digestion, so nearly all were cooked.

Less easily accessible, and hugely expensive, was sugar, along with condiments such as pepper, cloves, cinnamon, and nutmeg that were traded over long distances. These were needed not only to spice up dishes but also often to disguise the taste of meat going off.

The medieval diet of course lacked potatoes and tomatoes, two of today's staple European foods, that were only introduced from the Americas in the sixteenth century

FEASTS

In a lord's great hall, the high table was set on a dais so that the privileged could look down at the other diners. A canopy was often used to mark the place of honor, and the person who sat there would be given the "upper crust," the horizontal slice off the top of a loaf of bread. Salt was presented in a large, elaborate dish, and those of high status sat "above the salt," while the lower status diners sat below the salt.

Instead of plates, people used trenchers, large pieces of bread. There were no forks and few spoons, and although most people carried a knife, it was usual to simply eat with the fingers after dabbling them in a bowl of water.

Since there were many courses portions were small, and the meal would often center around one spectacular dish, perhaps a roasted bird with all its feathers replaced so it would seem to be whole and alive. The earliest British cookbook comes from the Middle Ages, and it contains the recipe for a four-and-twenty

Above: An outdoor banquet in the eleventh century.
Left: A French noblewoman of the 15th century dining with her household. The minstrels' gallery is in use for entertainment, and the servants wear shoes with extremely long points.

blackbird pie, made famous in the nursery rhyme. A giant pie was baked, with smaller cooked pies inside for each diner (the crusts were not eaten). On top of these live birds were placed, so that when the main crust was lifted in the dining hall, the birds would dramatically fly out.

Many dishes were used to entertain and amaze: meat might be disguised as fruits, or fishes as vegetables, and as well as shaping and moulding the food, a skilled cook would use plants such as parsley, rose petals, or violets to color the dishes.

SUBTLETIES

A feast might climax with the presentation of a subtlety, an elaborate sugar creation of a fantastic animal or other shape. Sometimes, these were not even edible but were simply to show off the cook's skills and the lord's largesse.

FESTIVAL FOOD

Many medieval festival foods and activities have survived:

- At Easter, painted hard-boiled eggs were given as prizes
- On Halloween, or All Soul's Eve, children would go from door-to-door begging for treats in the form of soul cakes
- The 12-day Christmas festival included wassails and games such as hunt-the-slipper

PEASANT FOOD

Unlike those who dined in the lord's great hall, the majority of medieval people had a very restricted diet.

Peasants seldom ate meat. In Britain, the very words for animals and meat show the divide between the Norman conquerors and the Saxon peasants who worked for them. For example, the animal is a cow, from the Anglo-Saxon, but its meat (served only to the upper classes) is beef, derived from the French word "boeuf." Similarly, sheep supplied mutton (from "mouton") and the swine or pig gave pork (from "porc") to the rich man's table. Poor families might keep chickens or a pig, but when slaughtered the porc would be salted or smoked, and made to last as long as possible.

Poorer families did not even have access to the wheat that they harvested. This was either milled for the lords, or was sent to market. Instead, barley and rye formed the peasants' breads, and the rest of their food was mainly vegetables or peas and beans, washed down with water or ale made from barley. However, at festivals even the poorest had a special, if humble, meal, in the form of Umble Pie (the umbles were the innards or tripe, which everyone could afford).

POACHING

Venison was usually forbidden, since deer-hunting was a recreation for nobles, who closely guarded their hunting areas, or "forests." Poachers were executed, and even children who snared rabbits in a forest might be killed.

Above: A suckling pig roasting on the spit: a medieval favorite.
Below: Goblets, plates, and a mortar and pestle of the period.

COSTUME AND DRESS

The simple tunic and hose of a working man; a high-waisted dress depicted in a stained glass window.

Unlike many regions, the European Middle Ages saw a wide range of costumes, but in general the medieval look meant a flared tunic, a robe, or tight hose. Clothing identified social status, and at times sumptuary laws defined which classes could wear certain clothes or colors. Lepers were supposed to wear white robes, and Jews and Muslims were meant to wear special badges.

In Western Europe the period began with many people adopting Roman costume – long, draped tunics, togas, dresses, or robes. When "barbarians" began to occupy the west, they brought with them their own styles for men: shorter, belted tunics with hose or leggings. These were sometimes nothing more than cloth strips wrapped around the legs.

CHURCH VESTMENTS

In the Early Middle Ages the distinctive costumes worn by Christian officiants developed, with shaven hairstyles known as tonsures, the loose, belted robe worn by the general clergy, and the ornate over-mantles worn by senior officials. Since churchmen were not expected to fight, they tended to fasten their cloaks at the center of their necks, rather than to one side.

The range of robes and vestments of churchmen was established during the Middle Ages.

This was the style that began to predominate in the Early Middle Ages, until only the clergy wore floor-length, long robes all of the time. The poorer you were, the shorter your tunic, since for practicality peasants seldom wore tunics below knee-length, whereas over time the wealthier elite began to adopt a longer over-tunic for leisure time. A formal outfit included a cloak or mantle, usually fastened at one shoulder (possibly to leave the sword arm free). All classes had a warm winter cloak, cheaply tied by the poor, or fastened with gold brooches by wealthy people to show off their status. The wealthy also had underwear of shirts and breeches.

Although there were regional differences, women's clothes were basically similar for centuries across Western Europe: a long, ankle-length dress with a slitted, laced bodice at the top. Again, additional layers such as an under-tunic and leggings depended upon wealth and status. However, a common feature of this period was introduced by medieval Christianity: the idea that married women should cover their hair. Many people wore a one-piece short cape and hood, called a "chaperon," which sometimes had a very long hanging tail, a liripipe.

In a style still seen today, peasant women wore headscarves and dresses of wool protected by an apron.

THE HIGH MIDDLE AGES
Wide sleeves and flaring skirts were introduced in this period, as well as stocking-like, separate hose that were laced to drawers. Another innovation was the men's doublet (a fitted, short top) and the coif, a hood knotted under the chin. By the end of the twelfth century women also adopted the wimple, a cloth wrapped around the neck and secured under a head veil. Their girdles or ceintures were often tasseled and elaborately knotted at the front. Crusaders discovered the need for the surcoat, a cloth over their armor to deflect the heat of the desert sun.

THE LATE MIDDLE AGES
In general, the later stages of the medieval period saw women's hemlines shorten, and men began to give up long over-tunics or

kirtles altogether in favor of the fitted doublet, also known as a cotehardie, jabon, pourpoint, or jaquetta. In order to preserve male modesty below these shorter tops, hose now became sewn as a single pair, held up by laces to the bottom of the doublet or to a belt. By 1350 some men were not even wearing a short tunic over their doublet and hose or breeches.

In the 1300s the chaparon hood shortened to become just a hat for men, but one that involved several complicated folds of cloth.

Women's underwear consisted of a chemise or smock, with knee-length hose. A gown or kirtle was worn over these, sometimes with long, fitted sleeves, and on top an over-gown, often belted, was worn. The hanging sleeves of these evolved into long, thin tippets by about 1400.

In northern and western Europe married women continued to cover their hair, sometimes with a snood or metal meshed caul or crespine, whereas in Italy women usually wore their hair uncovered, using ribbons or pearls for adornment.

In the 13th century the sleeveless tabard, just a rectangle with a hole for the head, was introduced, and in 1380, the high-collared, full robe with extremely trailing sleeves, the *houpeland*, appeared. This evolved into the standard wear of the professional classes, and eventually became the academic robes still seen today at universities.

In the fifteenth century some *houpelands* had big, bagged sleeves. Other changes included the woman's waistline rising while many gowns saw the neckline drop in a 'V' to show the top of the kirtle or a specially made *partlet*.

Headdresses became quite fantastic. In general women carried their hair on top, held up by the crespine, and the *hennin*, a wire-framed cone covered in fabric with a veil hanging off it, became popular. Huge horned or heart-shaped headdresses also appeared.

Fifteenth-century male dress saw fashionable young men wear ever shorter doublets with codpieces, even while the elders continued to wear robes. Most men wore colorful clothes (more flamboyant than women's finery), but plain, all-black suits were

In the Late Middle Ages parti-colored or *mi-parti* clothes were introduced, with items made of two different colors or fabrics. In particular, the legs of hose would be different colors.

Top: The kneeling man is wearing a full mi-parti suit.
Above: Liripipe: A huntsman wears a short cape with the long-tailed hood, the liripipe.

also introduced, possibly by Philip III (the Good), duke of Burgundy from 1419 to 1467.

MATERIALS

Wool was the most common material for medieval clothing, available to all classes although peasants would have had rough, home-spun. It takes dyes well and wears well.

Linen (woven from the flax plant) and hemp were also common. Linen could be bleached in the sun, was an easily laundered material, and could be made extremely fine and soft for the better off. Velvet was worn by those who could afford it, and silk and brocades were available to the wealthy when long-distance trade took place and the Silk Road from China could be traversed. Cotton was also imported from Egypt.

All sorts of furs were used for coats, and even poor people would have had rabbit fur to hand. Ermine became associated solely with royalty, and was worn with pieces of a black fur sewn in amongst the white for contrast.

Although woodblock printing of cloth was available by 1400, most decoration was provided by embroidery or the inclusion of pearls and other previous stones.

SHOES

A feature of fourteenth-century footwear was the extremely long, pointed toes of fashionable shoes. To keep shoes out of the muck, both men and women would tie on thick wooden pattens or clogs when walking outside. Shoes were not shaped for left or right feet, but were made to fit either foot.

BYZANTINE COSTUME

Somewhat conservative in their dress, the clothing of the Byzantines did not change nearly as much as that of Western Europeans. Roman togos evolved into long "tunicas" accompanied by an over-robe and a cloak, all of them highly colored and patterned.

Men's long, pointed shoes and high hats of the 1400s. While most men are wearing doublets, different types of robes are still worn.

MEDICINE IN THE MIDDLE AGES

Medicine in the early medieval period was hardly changed from that known by the Greeks and Romans. The sources were mainly Hippocrates of Kos, (born around 460 BCE), the "Father of Western Medicine" who gave his name to the famous Hippocratic Oath, and Galen of Pergamon (born around 129 CE), a Roman physician-surgeon and philosopher of Greek descent who contributed to the understanding of anatomy, pathology, physiology, and neurology. Translations of Arabic texts also added greatly to medieval medical knowledge, especially since the Arabs had contact with cultures of Africa, China, and India along long-distance trade routes. These Arabic and classical sources of theory and practice influenced western medicine for almost 2,000 years.

From these sources physicians received the concept of four humors or metabolic agents, which dominated medicine all the way through the medieval period until the early modern period. Medical conditions were diagnosed, appraised, and treated in accordance with these humors: yellow bile, phlegm, black bile, and blood, corresponding to the four elements of the natural world: fire, water, earth, and air. Medieval alchemists also acknowledged these four elements as being at the heart of all matter, and the magic arts had a role to play in medieval medicine. Although the idea of humors seems an almost holistic medical practice, superstition and religion also dictated how illness was perceived and treated in medieval Europe.

SUPERSTITION AND ALCHEMY

Superstition was part and parcel of medieval medicine. Prayers and incantations plus astrology and other forms of divination would accompany bloodletting with leeches, herbal poultices and potions, and basic surgery – without anesthetics – for cataracts, amputations, and bone-setting. Charms and holy relics were evoked, while gemstones were thought to have healing powers.

At first alchemists were believed to be wise, learned men and women, offering cures and magic potions. These early scientists were searching for the philosopher's stone, a supposed material that offered eternal life and also had the power to turn base metals into precious gold. Mixing magic and chemistry, alchemists did discover several useful substances, but many of them sold worthless or even dangerous products, and over time alchemists became dismissed as charlatans and conmen.

As the Middle Ages progressed, hospitals became attached to monasteries and priories. The literate monks translated Classical and Arabic texts, grew medical herbs and plants, and experimented with anesthetics using plants such as belladonna and hemlock. This was often as fatal as the original problem, and in the early 1300s the pope forbade monks from practicing surgery.

Only the wealthy had access to physicians; the majority had to rely on barber–surgeons, who were largely illiterate and had served apprenticeships to learn how to shave, cut hair, and perform surgery. The red-and-white striped pole that is still the barber's shop sign is said to be based on red for blood and white for bandages. Farmers were sought out for ailments such as tooth-pulling and cataract removal. Believing that illness was a disease of the soul, many did not go to surgeons or apothecaries, relying instead on curing their soul and repenting their sins by prayer and pilgrimage. There were also local "wise women" who had knowledge of herbs and midwifery.

By the tenth century the use of leeches in medicine had become a craft of its own, with some Anglo-Saxon manuals giving precise instructions. The word leech means healer, coming from Arabic and Indian roots. A vein would be cut and

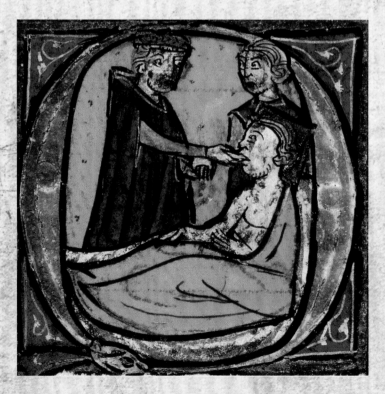

Left: Hippocrates treating a patient. He was one of the major sources for medieval doctors.

the leeches applied to draw off blood. Poultices and salves with vinegar, honey, and the appropriate herbal concoctions would be applied, and potions drunk.

ḦERḄAL ṂEDIȻIṆE

This hardly varied from the Greek and Roman remedies which stretched back to Ancient Egypt and the Middle East. It included:

Mint, yarrow, and myrrh for wounds

Archilla for battle wounds

Horewood for coughs and colds

Liquorice and comfrey for lungs

Wormwood, mint, and balm for stomach and vomiting

Certain illnesses and injuries, such as leprosy and bubonic plague, were seen to be a punishment from God. Ironically,

Above: A doctor receiving patients at his home.

Crusaders returning from the Holy Land brought leprosy and plague back with them. They were also responsible for epidemics of typhus, smallpox, and other infectious diseases for which there were no cures.

Although there was no understanding of viruses and bacteria, it was known that silver had protective properties, and the successors to the Knights Templar, wealthy Knights Hospitaller who were attached to the hospital in Jerusalem, carried silver plates and cups. Rich nobles used silver cups and plates to protect them from illness.

By the twelfth century there was a greater understanding of the natural world. A wider view of cosmology and science came with the translations of Ptolemaic astronomy and Aristotelian

Above: Victims of the Black Death lie dying with raised buboes.
Right: In despair at the horrors of the Black Death and other plagues, processions of flagellants would walk barefoot, whipping themselves, and praying to God for help.

logic, and in the twelfth and thirteenth centuries the number of apothecary shops increased, selling remedies along with astrological and alchemical consultations.

LEPROSY

From about the year 1000 lepers were barred from normal society. Many towns banned them, and in several parts of Europe lepers were required to live – and die – in special colonies. Otherwise, they had to wear special clothes identifying themselves as "unclean" or ring a bell to warn healthy people away.

Untreatable until the advent of modern medicine, leprosy meant inevitable disfigurement and an early, painful death. It was rampant for centuries, but declined during the later Middle Ages.

PLAGUE

Bubonic plague is carried by fleas that infest black rats, and rats were everywhere in the Middle Ages, on board ships, in houses, and in barns. Plague epidemics quickly crossed from country to country. Once bitten by a flea and infected, a human being

Left: A leech happily sucking blood. Blood-letting was used in an attempt to cure several illnesses.
Below: Leprosy was incurable apart from divine intervention. Here St. Francis of Assisi performs a miracle and cures a leper.

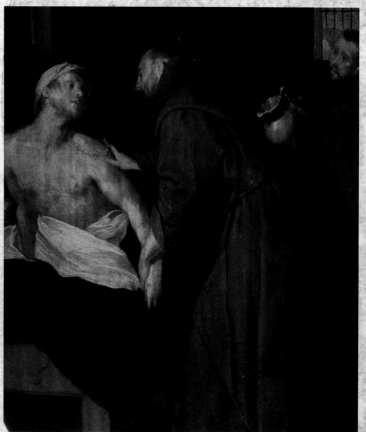

can easily spread the disease, since when it reaches the lungs and becomes pneumonic plague the victim coughs and sneezes, spraying the bacteria around.

Characterized by swollen, dark buboes or lymph nodes which probably gave the name to the 1347 epidemic the Black Death, plague was nearly always fatal, with death occurring just days after the first symptoms appeared. Outbreaks were commonplace during the Middle Ages, but the Black Death was particularly vicious, killing about 75 million people in Europe and the Middle East.

About a third of the population of Europe died. Whole villages and families were wiped out, and the epidemic, which raged until 1351, changed the face of medieval Europe. Feudalism was particularly affected, since many estates were left with not enough peasants to do the work. As a result, workers suddenly found that they were in demand, and many were enticed away from their homes to serve a new master. Their bounty was short-lived, however, since in England a 1351 decree capped wages at the 1348 level, and reinforced the right of lords to control peasants' movements.

Resentment at this feudal demand contributed to the Peasants' Revolt of 1381. More short-term results of the Black Death were a food shortage, since harvests were left abandoned in the fields; inflation; a shortage of trained, literate priests; a transfer of land and wealth, often benefiting just a few survivors; and a shift in some estates to sheep farming rather than crop-growing.

In 1377 Venetians tried to stop a plague outbreak by requiring ships to wait 40 days before anyone could disembark at ports. The Italian for 40 is "quaranta," giving rise to the term quarantine.

Plague epidemics continued in Europe until the seventeenth century, although none had such an impact as the Black Death.

OTHER DISEASES

Influenza and syphilis were other common diseases of the Middle Ages. A form of tuberculosis known as "scrofula" was widespread, and sicknesses caused by poor hygiene such as dysentery (the "bloody flux") were experienced throughout Europe. Malaria, or the ague, was found in southern Europe and also in marshy areas such as eastern England, and in the fifteenth century smallpox rampaged through the continent. There were regular outbreaks of ergotism, or "St. Anthony's fire," a poison caused by fungus on grain.

SWEATING SICKNESS

Also known as the "English sweat," this mysterious illness was first recorded amidst the army of Henry Tudor (VII) in 1485. It made several appearances over the next couple of centuries, then disappeared as suddenly as it had arose. As well as excessive sweating, victims experienced erratic breathing, nausea, and anxiety. The only cure was to lie down and wait for a recovery!

The title page of Italian doctor Mondino de Luzzi's *Lesson in Anatomy*. Born around 1270, he promoted public dissections to improve medical knowledge.

DANCING MANIA

Another unidentified medieval illness caused sufferers to dance wildly, with huge leaps, while screaming and frothing at the mouth. Eventually they would collapse in exhaustion, but would then jump up again and resume dancing. Perhaps a hysterical illness, like sweating sickness it arose, infected people throughout Europe, then disappeared. Dancing mania was sufficiently commonplace that musicians wrote special pieces that were played when sufferers were dancing.

SCIENCE, PHILOSOPHY, AND LEARNING

For most of the Middle Ages scholarship and education was the domain of the Church. Libraries were found almost exclusively in monasteries or other religious establishments, and some monasteries gained a reputation as centers of scholarship, attracting enquiring minds from around the continent. Nearly all the great medieval philosophers and scientists were members of one of the religious orders.

Greek was the language of scholarship in the late Roman period and classic Greek texts were held to be the wisest of all, but with the fall of Rome Europeans found themselves cut off from this source of knowledge. Aristotle, Euclid, and others were known only in fragments, part-translations into Latin, or commentaries. Although Europeans did make their own inquiries into the natural world, anyone who wanted to explore the classics was in a frustrating position.

ARAB TRANSLATIONS AND PTOLEMY

From the latter half of the eleventh century a new source of classic texts arrived via the Arab world. In Baghdad the caliphs had sponsored a House of Wisdom, which translated texts from around the world and encouraged scientific investigations. Arabic translations of the Greeks began to filter to Europe, and enterprising monks went into Arab lands in search of more information.

Gerard of Cremona, born in Italy around 1114, was one of them. In 1085 Alfonso VI of Castile had conquered

Left: Raphael's drawing of the philosophers Zoroaster and Ptolemy.
Right: A translation of Aristotle's Politics, Economics, and Ethics.

Toledo from the Muslims, but instead of destroying the city's infrastructure, as was common at the time, he allowed Muslims and Jews to stay, and encouraged scholars to use Toledo's famous libraries. Gerard went in search of a copy of Ptolemy's *Almagest*, an influential work on astronomy that was known only in fragments in Europe. He found what he sought, but stayed in Toledo to translate from the Arabic 87 texts including Euclid's *Geometry*, the *Toledan Tables*, the fullest set of astronomical data then known, and many Arab treatises on science.

Ptolemy's *Almagest* was the basis of Europe's understanding of the physical universe until the Renaissance. His impact was not so much his theory – that the sun and other planets revolved around the earth, which was the center of God's universe – but his *model* of a working universe. He provided a geometric framework using astronomical constructs to explain how the planets move and why certain phenomena can be seen in the heavens. Now, for the first time, European scholars could see in full how he had reached this model.

Ptolemy was wrong, but his geocentric theory, that the sun revolves around the earth, was supported by the

Above right: God surrounded by the zodiac. In the same way, earth was seen as being surrounded by "shells" containing the planets.
Below right: Scheme for a medieval water and vapor bath.
Below left: Alchemists were early scientists who also used magic and mysticism to search for truths. Often they sought the Philosopher's Stone that would give them eternal life and turn base metals into gold.

Church. Not until 1543 was an alternative model offered by Nicolaus Copernicus, who showed that the earth revolves around the sun.

Other major texts translated from the Arabic included the influential medical encyclopedias of Rhazes and Avicenna, and writings by the great Greek philosopher-scientist Aristotle.

ARISTOTLE

Ptolemy provided an explanation, but Aristotle was probably the greatest exponent of the geocentric theory of the universe. He argued that everything on earth was made up of the four classic elements: earth, air, fire, and water, and was forever changing. The heavens, however, consisted of a fifth, perfect element, aether, and did not change. He viewed the universe as a series of concentric spherical shells around the earth, each shell containing one of the planets. On the outside, in a fixed, unmoving shell, lay the stars.

Just as important as his cosmology was Aristotle's introduction of a formal logic giving rules for correct reasoning and deductive inference. He inquired into just about every field of the natural world, offering scientific and philosophical theories and writing copiously, and when his works were rediscovered in Europe they inspired an unprecedented surge in scientific inquiry and logical philosophy.

Aristotle's cosmology aligned perfectly with the Christian view of a perfect universe centered around God's creation of earth, and Aristotle's views became the accepted theory of the universe. Ironically, when scientists later began to question some of Aristotle's scientific statements, the Church took this as an attack on Christian faith itself.

ST. THOMAS AQUINAS AND SCHOLASTICISM

One of Europe's great intellectual movements arose from the attempt to reconcile Aristotelian logic with Christianity, and to prove the viability of the Bible through reason. There were many great thinkers in this so-called Scholastic movement, but one of the most influential was Thomas Aquinas.

Born in Italy in 1225, Thomas Aquinas studied under one of Medieval Europe's other great philosophers, Albertus Magnus, Albert the Great. Albert's systematized writings on Aristotle helped spread understanding of the Greek's ideas, and he was also called "Doctor Universalis" because of the range of subjects he contributed to.

Aquinas took up the mantle of proving that logic was compatible with Christianity, and showed how truth arrived at by faith can be in harmony with truth arrived at by reason. Both, he said, are gifts of God. Aquinas wrote perhaps 8 million words of Christian philosophy, and was so influential that his writings became official doctrine of the Roman Catholic Church. He was made a saint in 1323.

**Above: St. Thomas Aquinas, pictured in triumph over his theological rival.
Below: St. Thomas Aquinas and Albertus Magnus flank Dante and Beatrice in the middle of Philipp Veit's 18th century painting.**

experimental scientific method, which was advocated in particular by the thirteenth-century Franciscan Roger Bacon. William of Ockham, another English friar, offered a foundation of the scientific method when he argued that people should seek certainty in knowledge. He is best known for Occam's (Ockham's) Razor, a scientific principle that the fewest assumptions and the simplest conclusion may well be correct.

Although the Middle Ages started with a lack of scholarship, by the end of the period scientific inquiry was in full flow. Knowledge of the natural world had increased not just because of the introduction of classic and Arab texts but because the spirit of inquiry had taken hold. New universities were educating professional men, and technology was being applied in practical fields such as shipbuilding and navigation. These would all help Europe begin to dominate the world in later centuries.

UNIVERSITIES

For the first part of the medieval period education took place in schools attached to churches, cathedrals, or monasteries. They were subject to religious authority, and taught a narrow range of subjects. In the eleventh century a new institution arose, a school run along guild lines, organizing teachers and students into communities, awarding degrees, and offering a certain amount of academic freedom. Sometimes these new schools were simply the old church school growing bigger and more diverse, so in some ways were a continuation of monastic education. The first such university (from a Latin word meaning, in general, a guild or body of people) was organized to teach law, and new institutions sprang up rapidly. Often towns or princes would support the university, recognizing the value of associating with a group of educated men.

Teaching was in Latin, and most studies would focus on the works of the classic writers, particularly Aristotle. However regional differences began to appear, and Italian schools

Bologna	1088
Paris (Sorbonne)	c.1150
Oxford	1167
Palancia	1208
Cambridge	1209
Salamanca	by 1218
Montpellier	1220
Padua	1222
Naples	1224
Toulouse	1229

FIBONACCI – THE FIRST GREAT MATHEMATICIAN OF CHRISTIAN EUROPE

In 1200 numerate Europeans mainly used an abacus to perform multiplication or division calculations. Roman numerals – I V X C etc – were still in use, and while it was fairly straightforward to apply them to basic addition and subtraction, it was highly difficult to perform multiplication with Roman numerals.

A few years later scholars and professional men were doing their sums swiftly and easily using the Hindu-Arabic numerals that we still use today. The transformation was the work of one man, Leonardo Fibonacci of Pisa, whose 1202 work *Liber Abaci* (*The Book of Calculating* or *The Book of the Abacus*) was a ground-breaking work of European mathematics. In it he argued convincingly for the adoption of the decimal Hindu-Arabic system, which included the concept of zero and a decimal point. He was not the first to write about this system, but part of his mathematical genius was to make math interesting, and he offered persuasive, practical, everyday examples of why his proposed system was simpler and more efficient than Roman numerals.

Fibonacci learnt about the decimal system from Arabs, who were assimilating ideas from China and India, as well as from classic Greek and Roman texts. Apart from changing the face of European counting, he made several contributions to number theory which were only really recognized centuries after his death. His most famous idea was the Fibonacci sequence, in which every number is the sum of the two preceding numbers. In the modern world this sequence is applied in fields as far apart as astronomy, music, botany, and psychology.

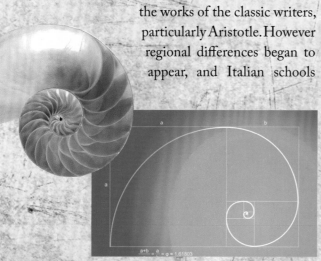

The Fibonacci sequence or number. Each square follows the Fibonacci sequence by being the sum of the two previous squares. The Fibonacci spiral is created by linking the opposite corners of consecutive squares with an arc. The nautilus shell is one example in nature that follows the sequence.

CRIME, PUNISHMENT, AND TORTURE

In Burgundy in 1457, the five-year-old boy Jean Martin was murdered. The suspect was quickly apprehended and brought to court. The suspect received a fair trial, being given ample opportunity to put forward her own defense, although, unable to talk, she was found guilty and condemned to death. There might seem nothing unusual about this case except for one strange thing – the suspect was a pig. The case was further complicated by the fact that the pig had killed Jean Martin in the presence of her six piglets. Because the boy's blood covered their skin, the judge ruled that the piglets were complicit in the murder and should be hanged alongside their mother.

Left: A gruesome punishment or "justice" scene.
Right: Hanging was a common form of execution.

Even monks misbehaved and were punished.

Such animal trials were common throughout the Middle Ages. In every European city all sorts of animals were brought to trial and punished if convicted. For larger animals, such as horses and bulls, special gallows were constructed for their execution. As odd as this might seem, animal trials were only part of the strange and brutal practices which made up medieval justice.

The Weregild was one of the oldest practices and was in use in northern Europe up until the twelfth century. In this system a value was placed on a life or a piece of property. If a person was killed or an item was stolen, the culprit had to recompense the victim or family of the deceased with an amount determined by the court.

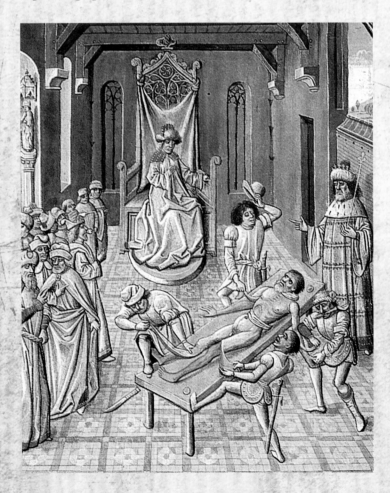

Compurgation was a judicial practice which enabled a defendant to establish his or her innocence by taking an oath. They were also required to bring forward another twelve persons to swear on oath to his or her innocence.

Left: The pillory was used to expose wrong-doers to the public. Passers by would often throw mud, rotten food, or excrement at the criminal.
Right: Executions were carried out in public.

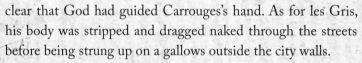

TRIAL BY ORDEAL

Although trail by judge or jury was commonplace, a person accused of a crime could prove his or her innocence by undergoing an ordeal. There were three main types of trial by ordeal: by fire, by water, and by combat. For trial by fire, the accused would have to walk over burning coals. If his or her feet received no injuries, they would be deemed innocent and let free. In trial by water, the accused had to dip their hand into a cauldron of boiling water to retrieve a stone. Once again, if no injury was visible, the accused was freed.

Trail by combat was almost exclusively the preserve of the aristocracy. In 1386, thousands of Parisians turned out to watch two men, dressed in full armor, fight each other to the death. Jean de Carrouges, a Norman knight, had accused his neighbor, Jacques les Gris, of raping de Carrouges' wife. The duel only ended when de Carrouges plunged his dagger through les Gris' helmet visor. At this, the audience erupted in applause, for it was clear that God had guided Carrouges's hand. As for les Gris, his body was stripped and dragged naked through the streets before being strung up on a gallows outside the city walls.

Another lesser-known form of trial by ordeal was corsening. For this, the accused would eat a piece of barley bread and cheese consecrated with a special prayer. If guilty, the accused would choke or vomit; if innocent they would be visibly nourished. In 1053, Earl Godwin of Essex, England choked to death after corsening. He was accused of murdering Alfred, the brother of King Edward the Confessor. His dramatic death was deemed to be conclusive proof of his guilt.

TORTURE

Torture was an extension of trial by ordeal, for it was a commonly held belief that God would protect the innocent, no matter how grave his or her suffering. Methods of torture included beating, blinding, boiling, bone-breaking, branding and burning, castration/genital mutilation, choking, cutting, disfigurement, dislocation, drowning, flagellation, whipping

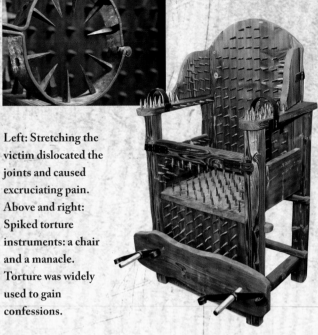

Left: Stretching the victim dislocated the joints and caused excruciating pain. Above and right: Spiked torture instruments: a chair and a manacle. Torture was widely used to gain confessions.

and beating, flaying, roasting, limb/finger removal, starvation, and tongue removal.

If the accused was found guilty prison was not an option. The jails were simply a place to confine a person until their sentence was passed. For minor crimes, a criminal would often be fined, while for more serious crimes such as theft or murder, corporal and capital punishment were always proscribed. A thief would be branded on the face or forehead, or have their ears or nose cut off.

Capital punishment varied from country to country. In England hanging was common but traitors were condemned to death by

being hanged, drawn, and quartered. This type of execution meant that the criminal was hanged until nearly dead, then was castrated and disembowelled, before being beheaded. The dead body was cut into four pieces, or quartered. Women were simply burnt at the stake, since it would have been indecent to expose their bodies in public! In the Italian Papal States criminals had their heads crushed with a mallet; in Eastern Europe impalement was popular. Such extraordinary violence seems inhumane, but at the time it was one of the means by which society functioned. For in a hard and brutal age, where life was short and often painful, the expectation was that judicial retribution should be equally violent and vicious.

Facing page: Torture equipment in a medieval dungeon.

Right (from left to right): Alive or dead, criminals were often exposed in cages; the "Iron Maiden," a popular form of torture. The victim was forced inside the spiked case and the door was swung shut, piercing the victim on all sides.

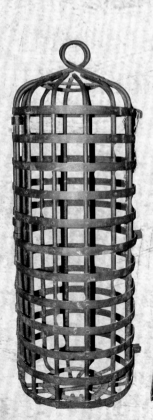

WITCHCRAFT

DEMONS

To the minds of medieval men and woman, God was all-powerful, yet his rule did not go unchallenged. In worlds unseen by mortal eyes, his nemesis, the Devil, waged a relentless war to corrupt the divine order. For the people of the medieval world, the Devil was no imaginary figure: he was real, he existed, and it was believed that he and his demons constantly sought to ensnare people. In the thirteenth century, a monk called Caesarius wrote a book, *Diagolus Miraculorum*, on the subject. He told how demons could take on human form, such as an ugly man dressed in black, or a Moor (African or Muslim), or even a handsome sailor should he wish to seduce a beautiful woman. More shocking than this, Caesarius said that demons could enter a person's body, making for themselves a home in the bowels where human waste was kept. Caesarius recounted how a five-year-old boy of his acquaintance swallowed a demon while drinking a glass of milk.

Demons were also thought to possess animals and even fruit. As late as 1602, a French judge by the name of Henri Bouget found

A demon from the illuminated manuscript the Books of Kells. Witches were thought to consort with demons.

an apple guilty of demonic possession. "It cannot be doubted that this apple was full of devils," he wrote of his encounter with the sinister fruit.

WITCHES

But it was witches, Satan's earthly followers, who posed the greatest threat to God's kingdom on earth. They were the hidden enemy, the Devil's fifth column. Witches were usually women, for it was believed that, being the weaker sex, women found it harder to resist the temptations of the Devil and his demons. Sex was often the cause of their downfall. Thomas Aquinas, the medieval theologian, believed that demons could not only mate with women, but could actually procreate with them. On the sabbats, or witches' feast days, witches flew through the night sky on the back of broomsticks to remote secluded areas such as mountain tops or forest clearings to call upon the Devil. After making love to him they would worship him as a living deity, whilst feasting on the flesh of babies. In return, the Devil would bestow upon his witches magical powers to use against all good Christians.

For most of the Middle Ages, there were few reported instances of witchcraft; the Church was far more interested in combating heresy. It was not until the fourteenth century, when the last European heresies had been suppressed, that witchcraft became a real issue. The first appearance of large cases was in southern France, parts of Switzerland, and northern Italy, areas which had previously been home to the Waldensian heresy.

Far left: The classic medieval image of women witches on broomsticks.
Left: Two witches casting a spell to make it rain.

WITCH-HUNTS

In 1320, Pope John XXII regarded witchcraft as an issue of such importance that he ordered the Inquisition to pursue and persecute witches. By the end of the century plague had wiped out a quarter of Europe's population, and it was at this point that witch-hunting become a hysteria that gripped virtually all of Europe. To aid inquisitors and witch-hunters, several guides were published. Peter Binsfeld's *Commentarius de Maleficius* (*Comments on Witchcraft*) suggested that the Devil left a diabolical mark on the skin of witches, such as a mole or birth mark. Binsfeld encouraged the use of horrible tortures to gain a confession, such as forcing women to sit on red-hot stools. He also claimed that if a woman showed fear during her interrogation then this was a clear sign of her guilt. Conversely, if she did not scream under torture this could also be interpreted as a sign of guilt since the Devil had the power to suppress pain.

In 1485, in the German town of Rothenbach in the Black Forest, a woman suspected of being a witch was brought to trial. The Judge, Count Furstenburg, ordered that she be tried by fire. The woman was forced to plunge her hand into a furnace and carry a red-hot coal for two paces. In fact the woman carried the coal for twice that length without incurring any discernible harm to her hands. Count Furstenburg declared the woman innocent but two Dominican friars, Heinrich Kramer and Jacob Sprenger, questioned his verdict. They claimed that the Devil, "by invisibly interposing some other substance" between the woman's hands, had been able to free his servant.

Witches continued to be hunted and burnt or hanged for another 150 years. With the slow rise of science, however, the calamities that sporadically shook Europe – a blighted harvest

Left: The ever-present fear of hell meant that anyone suspected of evil was harshly dealt with.
Right: Witches handing babies over to the Devil, to eat or to steal their souls.

or a plague – could be explained in rational terms, and there was no longer a need to idenfity and punish a scapegoat. Superstition faded along with belief in witchcraft, sorcery, and the Devil.

It was thought that most witches were women, and those accused would often be the most marginal and vulnerable, such as old widows.

With the decline of the Roman empire and migrations of Germanic tribes into formerly Roman lands, cities and towns all but disappeared, wiping out the large demand for goods that urban inhabitants had. In any event, long-distance travel became unsafe, and the old trade routes that had linked the Mediterranean with northern Europe were no longer used.

However even in the "Dark Ages" of the early medieval period trade took place. Pedlars traveled from village to village bringing goods from a short distance outside the local region, and small, traveling trade fairs were held regularly, enabling peasants to buy and sell their surplus products or crafted items. Barter was the most common form of exchange.

MARKETS AND TOWNS

Although many towns were based on old Roman cities, a great many new ones emerged because they had become the local market centers, where, instead of moving around, the merchants and artisans offered regular markets in the same spot. Flemish centers such as Bruges and Ghent developed in this way from becoming centers of the flourishing wool trade. In the tenth and eleventh centuries the populations of these market centers grew, until by the twelfth century they had become towns with individual identities, city walls and local administration, and were pressing for autonomy from the local lords. Only in that century did long-distance trade and a merchant class develop to any great extent, and with this economic revival prosperous towns and cities grew even faster, changing the face of Europe.

Since towns were usually centers for trade, they had to maintain close links and good relations with the manufacturing base around them, such as sheep farmers for the wool trade. Alternatively, if a town was the center of an import industry, then easy contact was needed with the towns of their export partners. Communications therefore improved, and travel of all forms became safer and more frequent. Coastal or riverside towns particularly began to flourish, and even while the new

Left: A group of pilgrims from the Ghent Altarpiece, a masterpiece by Flemish painters Hubert and Jan van Eyck. Pilgrimages would have been the only reason many medieval people took to the roads.
Below: A 10th-century Anglo-Saxon map indicating the relative directions of Africa (to the south) and Asia (to the east).

urban poor were as desperate as the rural poor, many merchants and artisans began to gain real wealth as a money-based economy returned.

The growth of manufacturing and trade helped erode the feudal system. As peasants saw the prosperity of artisans in cities they were drawn to leave their humble rural plots. It was often possible for peasants to buy their "freedom," and at times when their lord was short of money this would be looked upon favorably. Ironically, many lords were willing to take money instead of workers because as the trade in luxury items grew, they needed cash for their new lifestyles.

LONG-DISTANCE TRAVEL

One of the major factors in the growth of long-distance trade was the Crusades. As western Europeans ventured into the Middle East they came into contact with life-improving items, from textiles and carpets to pepper and other spices. The Arab world had been trading with the Far East and with Africa for centuries, and renewed contact with goods coming from so far away sparked a desire for new trading products in Europe.

Italian cities particularly profited from traffic across the Mediterranean, with Pisa, Genoa, and Venice becoming wealthy and powerful. As well as spices and textiles, pearls, perfumes, even paper from Egypt were brought to Europe in exchange for gold, silver, iron, wine, wool, and oil. Occasionally, even more exotic goods were traded: silk from China and gemstones or even animals from Africa.

Despite the growth of towns, large trade fairs continued until the later Middle Ages. Lasting for weeks, they were licensed by monarchs, and took place just once or twice a year. The four biggest in England in the thirteenth century were at Boston, Northampton, St. Ives, and Winchester, but the main center of long-distance trade in the twelfth and thirteenth centuries was the giant fairs held in Champagne, France.

Urban merchants hated these fairs, and did all they could to discourage them and to attract the business for themselves. By the end of the period the great fairs had indeed diminished in importance, possibly because with the use of a compass, sea routes became more popular.

Travel whether by land or sea was dangerous. Most merchants hired guards and traveled in large convoys to discourage bandits, slavers, or pirates. Their bases in foreign lands were often fortified, such as the Hanse in Novgorod, Russia and the Italian outposts in the Middle East.

PILGRIMS

Most people only traveled far from their homes if they went on pilgrimage to national sites such as Canterbury in England, or to the great centers of Christianity – Rome, Santiago de Compostela in Spain,

Above: Marco Polo and his relatives present a letter from the Pope to Kublai Khan.
Below: Merchants carried a small set of scales to weigh not just goods but also foreign coins in order to judge their value.

and Jerusalem. Pilgrims began to use standard routes, and these became the first regular long-distance roads since the Roman empire. When trade began to expand in the twelfth century the traders naturally followed these established roads, but soon began to forge new ones through mountain passes, improving communications throughout Europe.

MARCO POLO

Few people made very long journeys themselves. Goods were usually taken only a relatively short distance to a market hub and sold to another trader who would then take them further along the route before trading them onwards and returning home with new products.

Those few who made long journeys became celebrities, and the most famous of them all was Marco Polo. He was not the first European to travel along the so-called Silk Road that stretched from eastern Europe to China, but he became the best-known after his account, *The Travels of Marco Polo* was published to great success.

Born in 1254 to a family of wealthy Venetian traders, Marco actually followed in the footsteps of his father and uncle who began to trade to the east, making longer and longer trips until they reached China, known to them as Cathay, in 1266. The Silk Road was actually a network of routes that crossed deserts, mountain passes, and outlaw-infested wilderness, and there were long periods of history during which it was simply too dangerous to travel through some of those lands. The safest period was when the Mongols ruled nearly all the length of the roads, and ruthlessly protected their trade routes from bandits during the thirteenth and fourteenth centuries.

The Mongol emperor of China, Kublai Khan welcomed the Venetians and asked them to bring some learned Europeans to his court. So, once back in Italy, they prepared another expedition, taking Marco and a group of friars with them. The friars turned back, but the Italians continued their journey, arriving in China in 1275. Marco became an official and an ambassador for Kublai Khan and had the opportunity to travel around China before returning home, via the sea route to the Middle East, in 1291.

The wealth and luxury he saw astounded the European, and his tales would in turn astound his later readers. Although his book was probably embellished by the man who wrote the account down, Marco's report of China's magnificence was accurate.

THE AGE OF EXPLORATION

Marco Polo's stories of the gold and silver to be found in the Far East had a direct impact on the later Age of Exploration or Age of Discovery. As ships and navigational methods became more sophisticated, sailors set off to find new trading partners or new routes to Asia, and even Henry the Navigator, the Portuguese prince who was interested in astronomy and the continent of Africa for its own sake, and who organized several voyages of exploration along the African coast, was at least partly inspired by mercantile ambitions. When, in the mid fifteenth century, the Ottoman empire prevented silks and spices from Asia from reaching Europe, there was an added need to find a sea route to Asia: Europeans had grown used to their long-distance imports.

When Christopher Columbus set sail in 1492 and "discovered" the Americas, he was actually trying to find a sea route to the East Indies. He had dreams of following not in Marco Polo's footsteps, as such, but certainly following Polo's adventures.

GUILDS

Merchants were amongst the first professions to band together into formal guilds. From their humble beginnings as mutual self-help societies, these became wealthy and powerful, rigidly controlling their particular trade or profession and exerting influence on towns and rulers.

Guilds protected both their members and the public. They imposed high standards of professionalism and demanded proper training, but set standard prices and wages and ensured that there was not too much competition for their members. For example, they would not allow a new baker to set up too close to an established business. Guilds also provided one of the few ways to insure oneself against sickness and old age, since they undertook to support any members who became poor or could not work.

The guild system included a formal unpaid apprenticeship to a master, followed by a period as a journeyman, which originally really did mean that the aspiring craftsman would journey to learn from other masters of the profession. When judged ready, the journeyman would face a test for full membership of the guild, the need to present a "master piece" to prove that he was worthy.

Most guilds set up a central "show room" for their members, and these evolved into the elaborate guildhalls of medieval towns. Their members' fees helped pay for increasingly elaborate buildings designed to show the wealth and prosperity of individual members and of the organization itself. Guilds were popular with rulers since they took on the responsibility of collecting taxes from their members, and in turn towns often received permission to run their own affairs as long as taxes were paid. In this way the formation of guilds helped create another new institution, the autonomous town that was run by its own members, not the local lord, bishop or king.

Amongst the benefits of membership in a merchant guild was extra protection on the roads, since they would organize armed caravans of traders to travel together and deter bandits.

BANKING AND COUNTING

More sophisticated trade meant that the old system of a talley stick became outdated. This involved notching a debt on a stick that was broken in half. Each partner in the deal took one half, and if there was any dispute the pieces could be matched together to show the whole record. Bankers began to offer more complex accounting systems with written records, bills of sale or of credit, and double-entry bookkeeping, giving rise to a demand for educated and trained men. Governments also took part in the new trade flow, making commercial treaties that guaranteed the mutual safety of merchants.

THE HANSEATIC LEAGUE

By around 1300 there was a main sea trade network linking European ports from England and Flanders (now part of Belgium) along the Atlantic coast to the Straits of Gibraltar, then along the Mediterranean to Venice and Genoa in Italy. Wool, a major export for northern Europe, went south along with timber, coal, lead, copper, and iron, while oil, wine, salt, and luxury goods from the Middle East such as silk traveled northwards.

But quite apart from this traditional north–south movement, a new trade network had been forming, this time from east to west amongst the north European cities and their merchant guilds along the Baltic Sea. This new network completely dominated north European sea trade and became so powerful it was able to wage wars on countries in order to protect its mercantile interests.

Known as the Hanse (meaning company), Hansa, or Hanseatic League, this was a federation of cities or sometimes just the merchant guilds in cities. Acting as a sort of über-guild, the League protected its members' economic interests, cleared the Baltic of pirates, and established a series of outposts where its merchants could trade.

The League grew out of thirteenth-century merchant alliances, particularly the 1241 agreement between the towns of Lübeck and Hamburg in Germany for mutual protection and profit. Other cities saw the advantages of trade pacts, and either signed up or formed other alliances. Finally, the Hanseatic League was formally founded in 1358,

run by a diet or parliament of members, and with three internal divisions also run by diets. Lübeck became its most prominent member, but all the towns and guilds that belonged to the League profited from the trade monopolies that it arranged. Lübeck and several other cities were "free," that is they were not under the authority of anyone except the Holy Roman Emperor himself, who usually left these Baltic outposts alone. So they were indeed free to make their own independent trade rules and networks.

Based on nothing except mercantile interests, the Hanseatic League was another indication of the breakdown of Europe's old feudal system.

Growing to a membership of about 160 towns and guilds, plus a few semi-independent branches, the League's success was due to its ability to apply a commercial boycott and blockade, and by the development of a new flat-bottomed Baltic cog with a central rudder, innovations that were perfectly suited for the Baltic Sea. In addition, the original agreement between Lübeck and Hamburg led to a near monopoly on trade from the teaming herring fisheries around Denmark.

For its members the League organized large, well-protected convoys, and set up trading posts for its merchants to use in cities as far apart as Novgorod in Russia, Bergen in north Norway, and London. The Baltic was not a trade in luxury or rare goods, but in basic commodities like herring: grain from the lands of the Teutonic Order, wine from the Rhineland towns, coal, timber, and furs that could go back and forth the length of the Baltic or further west to the North Sea. The profit came from regular, bulk, and safe trade, and brought prosperity to its members for centuries.

The League was horrified in 1341 when Denmark managed to defeat part of its fleet in a disagreement over the herring rights, but reversed the tide in 1368–70 and went on to tighten its stranglehold on north European trade. It went into decline only in the late fifteenth century, when England and Russia closed down their respective outposts, the herring spawning grounds moved to the North Sea, England and Dutch ships began to improve, and internal rivalries began to destroy all hope of continuing cooperation.

Dietmar von Aist, a German love poet, woos his lady while disguised as a pedlar. Goods were carried on heavily laden packhorses.

THE WORLD DURING THE EUROPEAN MIDDLE AGES

Given that the Middle Ages actually covers a long time-span, it is not surprising that in other parts of the world society and affairs did not stand still. China is an example of a country that saw as many ups and downs as did European nations during the medieval centuries.

For much of the period China far surpassed Europe in terms of sophisticated art and technology. Printing, porcelain, and gunpowder were just three of the cultural advances the Chinese had long before others. The Tang dynasty, from 618 to 907, was a particularly glorious period which saw China influence other Asian countries.

Then the Mongol khans began to dominate huge swathes of Asia and eastern Europe. Kublai Khan conquered China in 1279, and it was not until 1368 that a new Chinese dynasty, the Mings, arose. They ushered in a new period of growth and prosperity, during which the Great Wall was extended and the Forbidden Palace built in Beijing.

India also saw great kingdoms arise, particularly under the Chola dynasty in the tenth and eleventh centuries.

THE MIDDLE EAST

In 570 Arabia saw a significant world event with the birth of Muhammad, who went on to become the prophet of Allah

Left: Guardian Lion Statue in the Forbidden City, Beijing, China. The palace complex was built from 1406 to 1420.
Right: The House of the Prophet (Nabawi) Mosque in Medina, Saudi Arabia.

(God) and found the religion of Islam. A few years after Muhammad's death in 622 the Arab armies began to conquer the Middle East and North Africa, and spread out to Asia and Africa, as well as to Spain and Portugal.

Timbuktu, now in Mali in Africa, became a major Islamic center of knowledge and trade, and other parts of Africa saw city-states that grew wealthy from trade in gold, copper, and ivory. Around 1350 Africa's first stone city, Great Zimbabwe, was built in the south. The center of a major empire, it flourished for 100 years. until it declined by1450.

THE AMERICAS

Great empires also rose and fell across the Atlantic. In Mexico the sophisticated Maya civilization declined by the end of the tenth century, but in its place came the Toltecs, the Aztecs, the Incas and others. All built impressive cities or structures, and had well developed societies.

For some periods of the Middle Ages, Europe was the rest of the world's poor relation. By the end of the period however, Europe came to dominate world affairs.

Above: The Chichen Itza pyramid in Mexico was used by the Mayans from the 7th through the 10th centuries.
Right: Around 1300 the era of statue-building began on Easter Island.

THE FUTURE: WHAT CAME AFTER THE MIDDLE AGES

There is no single cut-off date for the end of the Middle Ages. Historians work with several different dates in the late fifteenth and early sixteenth centuries, and many use the fall of Constantinople to the Ottoman Turks in 1453 as a cut-off point. But however vague historians are about the actual end of the medieval period, there are some events that are widely accepted to have taken place shortly *after* the era, and which helped define the early Modern Period that slowly emerged from the Middle Ages:

* The Renaissance – although this began in Italy in the fourteenth century while much of the rest of Europe was still in the grip of the Middle Ages, it flourished throughout the continent after the medieval period. Apart from the glorious arts of the period, the re-discovery of classical knowledge and the expansion of scientific enquiry led to the European Enlightenment and an explosion of science and philosophy throughout the continent. Artists such as Leonardo da Vinci and Michaelangelo flourished

* The Protestant Reformation – instigated by Martin Luther (1493–1546) in 1518 when he supposedly posted on a church door at Wittenburg his protests against Catholic corruption. This led to the eventual division of the western Christian church

Above: Suleiman the Magnificent at the Battle of Mohacs, 1526, when the Ottoman empire was at its height.
Below: St. Basil's Cathedral, Moscow, Russia, begun in 1555.

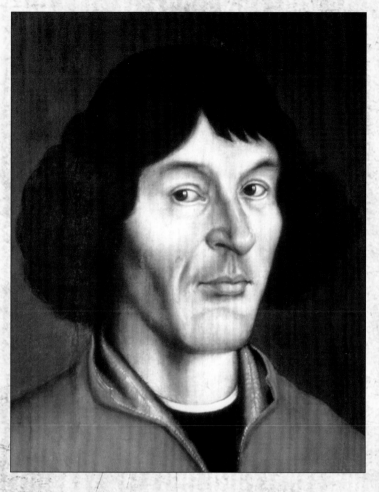

* The Age of the Tudor monarchs in England, when Henry VIII and Elizabeth I made England one of the world's pre-eminent powers
* The Thirty Years' War in Germany that devastated central Europe
* French Wars of Religion between Catholics and Huguenot Protestants
* The Dutch Revolt against Spain
* European colonization of the Americas and parts of Africa and the Far East, a process that completely changed the face of the world and led to centuries of European dominance. It also spread Christianity around the world
* The beginnings of the slave trade from Africa to the Americas, and the African diaspora

Feudalism died out completely in almost every part of western Europe, and individuals began to seek more autonomy and choice in their lifestyles. Cities grew rapidly as more and more people chose to leave the countryside, trade became truly global, the embryonic middle class became a permanent feature, and the capitalist system began to emerge.

Above left and right: Polish astronomer Nicolaus Copernicus and Italian scientist Galileo helped change our understanding of the universe. Right: Leonardo's Mona Lisa, painted in 1503.

BIBLIOGRAPHY

Alford, John A., ed. *A Companion to Piers Plowman*. University of California Press 1988.

Ashdown, Charles H. *Armour and Weapons in the Middle Ages*. Harrup & Co 1925.

Baker, Peter S., ed. *Beowulf: Basic Readings*. Garland 1995.

Bartlett, Robert. *Medieval Panorama*. Oxford University Press 2001

Beadle, Richard, ed. *The Cambridge Companion to Medieval English Theatre*. Cambridge University Press 1994.

Bishop, Morris. *The Middle Ages*. Houghton Mifflin Harcourt 2001.

Bredero, A.H. *Christendom and Christianity in the Middle Ages*. Eerdmans Publishing Company 1994.

Brewer, Derek and Jonathan Gibson, eds. *A Companion to the Gawain-Poet*. Cambridge University Press 1996.

Brooke, C. and R. *Popular Religion in the Middle Ages*. Thames and Hudson 1984.

Cantor, Norman. *The Civilization of the Middle Ages*. HarperCollins 1994.

Carruthers, Mary, *The Book of Memory*. Cambridge University Press 1990.

Chalton, Nicola, ed. *Philosophers: Extraordinary People Who Altered the Course of History*. Basement Press 2008.

Chenu, M.D. *Nature, Man and Society in the Twelfth Century*. University of Toronto Press 1997.

Chesterton, G. K. *Aquinas, the Dumb Ox*. Dover Publications 2009.

Chesterton, G. K. *St. Francis of Assisi*. Image 1987.

Christiansen, Eric. *The Northern Crusades*. Penguin 1998.

Cosman, Madeleine Pelner. *Medieval Holidays and Festivals*. Piatkus 1984.

Curtius, E. R. *European Literature and the Latin Middle Ages*. Pantheon 1953.

Dawson, Christopher. *The Making of Europe*. Meridian 1965.

Dawson, Christopher. *Religion and the Rise of Western Culture*. Sheed and Ward 1950.

Delouche, Frédéric. *Illustrated History of Europe*. Cassell 2001.

Dunn, Diana. *War and Society in Medieval and Early Modern Britain*. Liverpool University Press 2000.

Dyer, Christopher. *Standards of Living in the later Middle Ages*. Cambridge University Press 1989.

Evans, Joan, ed. *The Flowering of the Middle Ages*. Thames and Hudson 1998.

Ferrante, Joan. *Woman as Image in Medieval Literature*. Columbia University Press 1985.

Fletcher, Richard. *The Cross and the Crescent: Christianity and Islam From Muhammed to the Reformation*. Penguin 2004.

Gilson, E. *Reason and Revelation in the Middle Ages*. Macmillan 1977.

Gilson, E. *The Spirit of Medieval Philosophy*. Scribners's 1940.

Gimple, Jean. *The Medieval Machine*. Holt, Rinehart and Winston 1976.

Grant, Edward. *Physical Science in the Middle Ages*. Wiley 1971.

Grover, Razia. *Cathedrals of the World*. Worth Press 2010.

Gurevich, Aron, *Medieval Popular Culture*. Routledge & Kegan Paul 1985

Hanawalt, Barbara A. *The Middle Ages*. Oxford University Press1998.

Haskins, C. H. *The Renaissance of the Twelfth Century*. Harvard University Press 1927.

Herlihy, David. *Women, Family and Society in Medieval Europe*. Berghahn Books 1995.

Holmes, George, ed. *The Oxford History of Medieval Europe*. Oxford University Press 2002.

Holmes, George, ed. *The Oxford Illustrated History of the Crusades*. Oxford University Press 2001

Holsinger, Bruce. *Music, Body and Desire in Medieval Culture*. Stanford University Press 2001.

Huizinga, Johan, *The Waning of the Middle Ages*. Penguin 2001.

Humphreys, Henry Noel and Owen Jones. *The Illuminated Books of the Middle Ages*. Bracken Books 1989.

Jones, Gwyn. *A History of the Vikings*. Oxford University Press 1968.

Keen, Maurice. *Chivalry*. Yale University Press, 1984.

Keen, Maurice Hugh. *The Penguin History of Medieval Europe*. Penguin 1968.

Knowles, David. *The Evolution of Medieval Thought*. Longman 1962.

Lewis, C.S. *The Allegory of Love*. Oxford University Press 1985.

Luscombe, David and Jonathan Riley-Smith, eds. *The New Cambridge Medieval History*. Cambridge University Press 2004.

MacArdle, Meredith, ed. *Scientists: Extraordinary People Who Altered the Course of History*. Basement Press 2008.Macdonald, Fiona. *The Middle Ages.* Raintree 2005.

McGuire, B. P. *Friendship and Community: The Monastic Experience, 350–1250.* Cistercian Publishing 1988.

Morgan, David. *The Mongols*. Blackwell 1986.

Mortimer, Ian. *The Time-traveller's Guide to Medieval England: A Handbook for Visitors to the Fourteenth Century*. Vintage 2009.

Nolan, Barbara. *The Gothic Visionary Perspective*. Princeton University Press 1977.

O'Meara, Thomas. *Thomas Aquinas, Theologian*. Notre Dame Press 1997.

Oakley, Francis. *The Medieval Experience*. Universisty of Toronto Press 1988.

Oakley, Francis. *The Western Church in the Later Middle Ages*. Cornell 1985.

Panofsky, Erwin. *Gothic Architecture and Scholasticism*. Meridiann 1957.

Patterson, Lee. *Negotiating the Past*. University of Wisconsin Press 1987.

Pearsall, Derek. *Old English and Middle English Poetry*. Routledge 1977.

Phillips, J. R. S. *The Medieval Expansion of Europe*. Oxford University Press 1988.

Pieper, Josef. *Scholasticism*. St. Augustine's Press 1960.

Pieper, Josef. *The Silence of St. Thomas*. St. Augustine's Press 1999.

Pirenne, Henri. *Mohammed and Charlemagne*. Meridian 1960.

Riley-Smith, Jonathan, ed. *The Oxford Illustrated History of the Crusades*. Oxford University Press 1997.

Saigal, Malini. *Castles of the World*. Worth Press 2010.

Smalley, Beryl. *The Study of the Bible in the Middle Ages*. Blackwell 1983.

Southern, R.W. *The Making of the Middle Ages*. Yale University Press 1964.

Strayer, R. *Dictionary of the Middle Ages*. Scribner 1982.

Sumption, J. *Pilgrimage*. Faber and Faber 1975.

The Middle Ages. Marshall Cavendish 1995.

Turville-Petre, Thorlac. *England the Nation*. Clarendon Press 1996.

Vauchez, Andre. *The Laity in the Middle Ages: Religious Belief and Devotional Practices*. University of Ntre Dame Press 1993.

Wallace, David, ed. *The Cambridge History of Medieval English Literature*. Cambridge University Press 1999.

Ward, Benedicta. *Miracles and the Medieval Mind*. University of Pennsylvania Press 1987.

White, Lynn, Jr. *Medieval Religion and Technology*. University of California Press 1978.

White, Lynn, Jr. *Medieval Technology and Social Change*. Oxford University Press 1962.

Whittock, Martyn. *A Brief History of Life in the Middle Ages*. Robinson 2009.

MAJOR MUSEUMS

Bork Viking Harbour, Skjern, Denmark

British Museum, London, England

Cluny Museum, Paris, France

Hungarian National Museum, Budapest, Hungary

Jorvik Viking Centre, York, England

Metropolitan Museum of Art, New York, USA

Museum of Art History, Vienna, Austria

Museum of the Middle Ages, Carcassonne, France

National Museum, Munich, Germany

National Museum of the Early Middle Ages, Rome, Italy

National Museum of the Middle Ages, Paris, France

Victoria and Albert Museum, London, England